D1301330

TO THEE WE DO CRY

A Grandmother's Journey through Grief

PAT MONAHAN

iUniverse, Inc.
Bloomington

To Thee We Do Cry
A Grandmother's Journey through Grief

Copyright © 2010 Pat Monahan

All rights reserved. No part of this book may be used or reproduced by any means, graphic, electronic, or mechanical, including photocopying, recording, taping or by any information storage retrieval system without the written permission of the publisher except in the case of brief quotations embodied in critical articles and reviews.

iUniverse books may be ordered through booksellers or by contacting:

iUniverse
1663 Liberty Drive
Bloomington, IN 47403
www.iuniverse.com
1-800-Authors (1-800-288-4677)

Because of the dynamic nature of the Internet, any Web addresses or links contained in this book may have changed since publication and may no longer be valid. The views expressed in this work are solely those of the author and do not necessarily reflect the views of the publisher, and the publisher hereby disclaims any responsibility for them.

ISBN: 978-1-4502-7172-1 (pbk)
ISBN: 978-1-4502-7173-8 (cloth)
ISBN: 978-1-4502-7174-5 (ebk)

Library of Congress Control Number: 2010916934

Printed in the United States of America

iUniverse rev. date: 11/17/2010

Tommy's last soccer triumph at a Virginia Beach tournament

8-29-98 — 12-17-07

Tommy

"HE LOVED ALL CREATURES GREAT AND SMALL"

Tommy having fun

DEDICATION

I dedicate this book to all our grandchildren, whose lives are clear signs of God's love. Thank you for all the special moments and hugs that you share with me. May you always feel God's light shining through each of you.

Our Precious Angels:
Kaitlyn and Kevin Monahan
Thomas, Christina, and Joey Quercia
Scott and Catie Monahan
Russell and Ryan Monahan
Craig and Christian Monahan
Kayla, Kathleen, and John Connolly
Kevin and Ashley McCue
Gabrielle Monahan
and Tommy, who lives in heaven

CONTENTS

PREFACE:
"Tommy"

By Ryan Hepworth

For the past few years, I have been working as a camp counselor for the Staten Island Institute of Arts and Sciences' "Earth Camp." The objective of the job is the following: "control a bunch of rowdy young kids, and at the same time, try to teach them a bit about nature." It's not easy and I don't get paid an exorbitant amount of money, yet I love doing it. Why do I love it? The reason I drag myself out of bed early on sweltering summer mornings and traverse Staten Island is because of the kids. Sure, a lot of them are wise guys who just don't care. The ones who are truly into it, though—the kids who go because they appreciate nature—make working through the dog days of August worth it. That was precisely the type of camper Tommy Monahan was.

Tommy was an energetic, inquisitive, and sometimes crazy nine-year-old whom I had the pleasure of instructing for the past couple summers. He was not like a lot of campers. He was one of those "special ones," the type of kid who would much rather be out backpacking in the deep woods than inside playing the Nintendo Wii all day. He was given the nickname "Steve Irwin Jr." by his peers due to his incredible bravery and love of nature and all its creatures. When I'd see this pint-sized, freckle-faced, crimson-haired connoisseur of nature run after a butterfly with his net, lift a heavy rock in search of salamanders, or dive for an Indian artifact on the ground, I couldn't help but chuckle and crack a smile. Tommy's antics and environmental zeal made me forget the fact that it was probably 100 degrees out and my skin resembled a dartboard due to all the mosquito bites I had gotten. He was destined to become a "lifer," the term used to describe those who spend many years in the camp, like yours truly. (I've been trekking through the forests of Staten Island since 1996.)

However, young Tommy Monahan will sadly never be given a chance to become a "lifer." His life was tragically cut short in a house fire on December 17, 2007. He died trying to save his beloved Yorkshire terrier Sophie from the fire, a testament to his incredible bravery and love of animals. I still remember getting the morbid news. It came in the form of a phone call from my mother while I was frantically studying for final exams, which had me cursing the day I was born. The terrible news stunned me. Tommy Monahan, "Steve Irwin Jr.," one of the truly exemplary campers, was now deceased. His death made me take a step back and reexamine my own life. It made me realize how fortunate and foolish I truly was. Here I was, still alive and well, attending a prestigious university, complaining about final exams—while only a borough away, the despondent Monahan family was mourning the loss of their son. Who was I to complain? Final exams may have made my life a living hell for a few days, but the loss of a child leaves a permanent void in one's life. There will be many more finals and all-nighters, but there will never be another Tommy Monahan.

Despite my receiving the news and subsequently seeing articles about the house fire, it still had not quite sunk in yet that Tommy had passed. It wasn't until I went to his wake that I finally realized I'd no longer be seeing him in Earth Camp. When I saw him on the last day of camp this past summer and we said our good-byes, little did I know that the next time I'd be seeing him, he'd be in a coffin. It was a harsh dose of reality, the kind of thing that would make even the toughest, most resolute man's eyes well up. As I gazed around the room, I could see and hear people crying. Family members, classmates, fellow campers—there wasn't a dry eye in the room. I could feel tears forming in the corners of my own eyes as I approached the casket, his little body lying there, clothed in his soccer uniform, surrounded by possessions that were so dear to him. It wasn't easy seeing a protégé of mine lifeless in a casket. He doesn't belong here, not now. He should be out salamander hunting, I thought to myself. Then I saw the pictures of Tommy, many of which were pictures of him in Earth Camp. He looked so happy and carefree, the polar opposite of how everyone at the wake obviously felt. Viewing those pictures made me feel a bit joyous again on an otherwise somber evening. I then knew that my seemingly mundane camp-counselor job was one of the things that made Tommy happy. I felt good knowing that I was a part of his short but fulfilling life. The number of people who showed up was astounding and a bit ironic. Tommy never got married, never had kids, never even finished grammar school. Yet the line of mourners stretched out of the funeral home and wrapped around the parking lot. It was as if the president decided to have his funeral on an obscure part of Amboy Road. I wasn't surprised, though. Tommy was just that special, a case study proving that it's quality, not quantity that matters. He got more out of his nine years on Earth than most people do out of ninety.

I realize that most of you unfortunately never had the opportunity to meet Tommy. He was truly an amazing kid, the kind of person you'd be proud to call a friend. As I'm writing this, he's probably watching over us all, chasing around nature's many extinct and deceased creatures, perhaps even teaching the late Steve Irwin himself a thing or two. My attempt to eulogize him, although from the heart, does not do him justice: Tommy was just too special to sum up in a few printed pages. Even if you've never met him, please keep him and his family in your thoughts and prayers this Christmas. His death is a tragedy, a reminder that we can lose the ones we love at any moment. Life is fragile; it can be snuffed out like a candle flame at any time, even at the tender age of nine. As young as I am, I've already lived two of Tommy's lifetimes. He'll never get the chance to hug his mother and father again, to hike in the woods, or play soccer—at least not in this world. Keeping that in mind, try to spend a little more time with the ones who care about you this Christmas. Whether it's hugging someone longer than usual or making that extra effort to be jolly, show the ones who love you that you love them, too. Godspeed, Tommy "Steve Irwin" Monahan. Earth Camp will never be quite the same without you.

Ryan...

Reprinted with permission of Ryan Hepworth. This eulogy was sent to Tommy's parents, Tom and Maria, by Ryan's mother.

Exploring Earth Camp

ACKNOWLEDGMENTS

This book would not have happened without the inspiration and guidance of the Holy Spirit. After much prayer and meditation, the words just flowed from my pen. After the first month of writing, I believe it was the Holy Spirit that woke me at three o'clock one morning with the title.

I thank Monsignor Peter Finn, who encouraged me to write a book when the time was right. Thank you, Maria and Tom, for always sharing Tommy and Gabrielle with us and encouraging this journey of mine despite the pain these words might cause. Your support and contributions have meant the world to me. My husband, Tom, has lovingly sacrificed a clean house and many home-cooked meals because of the time I spent working on this labor of love. Thank you for blessing me with seven of the most special children God put on this earth. Thank you also for your unconditional love and tiring hours transcribing my notes.

Thank you, Monsignor Edmund Whalen, for your guidance, prayers, and encouragement to put my words "out there." I don't know what I would have done without my brilliant, computer-expert daughter Terry Quercia for the days she and her daughter, Christina Quercia, spent putting my work on the computer in a professional format. If it wasn't for Terry, I never could have responded to the recommended changes from the editing department to begin the publishing process. Thanks go to my daughter, Melissa Connolly, for pinch-hitting that long night of typing. Many thanks go to our children and their spouses: Kevin and Linda Monahan, Scott and Patti Monahan, Russell and

Anita Monahan, Craig and Sharin Monahan, Tommy Quercia, and Wally Connolly for all your love and support.

My brother, Dennis Nisi, and sisters, Linda Wolfgram and Kathy Leighton, have been a constant source of support even though they live in Texas and California. Their presence at the wake and the funeral and ongoing phone calls have encouraged and supported me on this journey.

Thank you seems inadequate to my proofreaders: my granddaughter Kaitlyn, a third-year Rutgers pre-vet student; Carolyn Oglio, the director of The Little Angels Program and professor at Wagner College; my friend and mentor Mary Ann Walsh; and my friend Betty Stroh. Thanks to Carolyn for putting my words into chapters for easier reading. Dolores Talley and friends in the Bereavement Support Group were always there to encourage my efforts. Many thanks go to all my friends at the YMCA and at daily Mass, who prayed for this process and my ability to reach others through this book. Your daily encouragement kept me going.

Last but not least, I thank my granddaughter Gabrielle Monahan (Tommy's sister) for creating this book cover. Her enthusiasm and efforts to honor her brother with her artistic abilities warm my heart.

Patricia Monahan

Introduction:
A Heartbreaking Journey

"So a mother comforts her child, so I will comfort you."
(Isaiah 66:13)

The death of our grandchild has been the most devastating event of our lives. When we heard there was a fire in our son's house, we couldn't begin to comprehend what was to follow. Trying to live our lives as good, Catholic, patriotic citizens who devote our lives to God, our family, and our community, we never imagined we would have to face the sudden, tragic death of such an energetic nine-year-old grandson filled with such love for life and for all of God's creatures. Our world as we knew it stopped as abruptly as a speeding train wreck. The pain and sorrow we had to face was beyond description. The overwhelming pain consumed our hearts and minds. The powerlessness of not being able to change the facts, stop the unending nightmares, nor take the pain from our son and his family, has been the worst journey of our lives. Our faith, our family, our church, and all the good people in our lives are what gave us the energy to fight our way through this dark, unending tunnel.

I began to journal as a way to cope with my emotions. I chose to print this journal hoping it might help other bereaved families find their way through identification, normalizing their struggle and bringing understanding and hope that life does go on. Our breaking hearts won't ever completely heal, but we can find the strength to move into life by facing the facts—one moment at a time. Our child has lost his only son without warning and with no success in his futile attempts to save him.

How do we help our son, Tom, move on? How do we help his wife, Maria, face her pain—or our eight-year-old granddaughter, Gabrielle, accept the death of her sidekick brother and their dog, Sophie? We thank God that Gabrielle, her older brother Kevin, and her older sister Ashley can help each other with the death of their brother, Tommy.

I pray that my readers have practiced fire drills with their families and treasure every moment they have with all their loved ones. I am so grateful I took so many pictures of all of our eighteen grandchildren. The precious moments we captured with Tommy are so helpful with the memories of those special events. Time with family is so important.

My husband, Tom, and I were married forty-nine years on April 4, 2008. We raised seven children with seven different personalities, who married seven spouses with seven different personalities, who had eighteen grandchildren with eighteen more different personalities. I consider us lucky to have all those differences. It is a challenge getting together for special occasions, especially since everyone is actively involved with their own individual lives. Somehow it works, especially with the grandchildren.

Christmas was oh so difficult, coming only six days after Tommy's funeral. I was so grateful our daughter, Terry, was still having Christmas at her house. Traditionally, Grandpa and I don't set up our live, tall, Christmas tree before the second week of Advent, since we don't want it dying before the Epiphany in January. However, this year, Grandpa set it up early. (There are no coincidences; God must have nudged Grandpa early.) He also put the lights on the tree, and I set up my mom's Christmas village along with the nativity we've had since we first married. Even after Tommy died, though certainly not in a festive mood, we couldn't forget the meaning of Christmas. As depressed and saddened as we all were, we awaited the birth of Jesus, knowing Tommy was spending his first Christmas in heaven. Do you know how sad that was? Yet we were so happy for him that he was at home with the Christ child amidst the animals in the stable.

We were so grateful that Santa came to visit Gabrielle on Christmas Eve. She was worried Santa wouldn't know where she lived now since Tom, Maria, and the children had moved in with us after the fire. Gabrielle and I sang "Happy Birthday" to Jesus on Christmas morning as she placed a candle and baby Jesus in each of our mangers. The only

Christmas ornaments on the tree were the few homemade ornaments from the grandchildren that I had on the tree the day Tommy died, along with ornaments people gave Tom, Maria, Gabrielle, Kevin, and Ashley. Grandpa and I also gave them the ornaments we had for each of them, as is our traditional gift each year. The tears on Christmas flowed like a river. Mass was also quite emotional, although we are so grateful to God for the birth of Christ. It is because he was born and died on the cross to save us all that we know our Tommy has everlasting life. We are so grateful to God for His gift of the Christ child.

I was thrilled when Gabrielle asked, "Grandma, are we were going to have our annual Christmas pageant on Christmas this year?" For the past twelve years, our family has a Christmas pageant with all the grandchildren. While the parents are having dessert after dinner, the grandchildren and I get out the costumes and props and decide who will be which character in the story of the first Christmas. One of the older grandchildren is the narrator, one helps out backstage, and the others participate.

"Yes, Gabrielle, we certainly will have the pageant," I assured her.

Gabrielle responded, "Great, can I be Mary this year?"

Traditionally it would be Kathleen's turn to be Mary this year. However under the circumstances, I responded, "Absolutely, Gabrielle, you will be Mary." It was good. She asked for what she needed.

There are times when some of the boys want to sit in the audience or just play with the dogs that are enlisted as "the sheep." I remember when Gabrielle was only eighteen days old, and she was Jesus that year. Her one-year-old brother, Tommy, reluctantly played a shepherd (escorted by his dad), even as he resisted the shawl he had around his shoulder. That year was hysterical because Tommy's "best buddy," his cousin Joey (who was three years old), was a king. During practice we used a doll as Jesus. During the show, as Joey came from behind Mary and Joseph, ready to present his gift to Jesus, he said out loud as he did a double take with his head, "Oh, wow, it's the real thing."

Well, here it is 2007, and Tommy is in heaven watching over this year's pageant. At her request, Gabrielle was Mary, and an excellent job she did. Her cousin Ryan was kind enough to be Joseph, with much reverence. Our faithful Kaitlyn and Christina expertly directed the actors, as dedicated Catie eloquently narrated. *Angel*ic Kathleen was perfection, and Joey and Kayla were serious and regal in their presentation of gifts as kings. Craig and Christian were escorted by their dad as shepherds, followed by their sheep (Scooter and Snowball). Johnny was Jesus, with the biggest smile on his happy face. Tommy's loss was felt by all, but the spirit of the pageant went on. We all knew his spirit was with us, and we felt the tears through our laughter.

We also felt his presence when we went to Woodloch Pines Family Resort in Hawley, Pennsylvania. Tom and Maria chose to stay home with Kevin and Ashley. It was too difficult for them to be at a family gathering: Tommy should have been there. Gabrielle was with us, however. She was looking forward to being with her cousins. Grandpa and I arrange for this as our yearly Christmas gift to the entire family along with a Christmas ornament. A roller coaster of emotions permeated that weekend. It wasn't fair to the children to cancel an event they looked forward to every year with great anticipation. However, we had to work hard to make it the best it could be. We all commented on Tommy arranging the most perfect weather we've had there in all the years we've been going. The weather was perfect for sleigh riding and walking in the snow. This was the first year I was able to make it up that steep snow hill in order to watch their sledding excursions from the top. I even went for my first snow tube trip down the hill. It was quite hysterical. Tommy's Aunt Linda tried diverting my tube as it sped down the hill, and his Aunt Patti had to grab my leg as I headed toward the wet creek.

All of us were out on the slope when our sons (Tommy's uncles Craig and Scott) spotted a field mouse running across our slope. The kids went wild. We all believed it was Tommy, or else he made that mouse run through us. Joey gently caught the mouse but soon set it free. As one of the young boys went to recapture the mouse, he buried himself in the snow—never to be seen by us again. It was a precious moment as we all spoke with Tommy.

When the uncles took the grandchildren through the woods, they came across a herd of deer after following their footprints. It was another sign that Tommy was with us that day. Uncle Craig spotted him watching us from afar periodically. It was a great weekend.

Tommy's death crushed each and every one of their hearts. His presence is sorely missed. The events surrounding his death are incomprehensible to process, especially for Tommy's siblings, cousins, and friends. We see and feel his presence at every gathering. Actually, I think it's quite interesting how we all feel his presence daily, no matter where we are individually. God works in mysterious ways, as many of us know. One thing we know for sure is that God has been there for us every step of the way.

St Francis of Assisi - Patron saint of animals and
the environment (Two of Tommy's passions)

GRANDMA'S JOURNAL

Grandpa, Tommy, and Grandma

CHAPTER *1:*
The Worst Night of Our Lives

"Blessed are those who mourn, for they will be comforted."
(Matthew 5:4)

I started this journal on Saturday, April 12, 2008, as I sat on our balcony overlooking the ocean on a cool, windy day. Our ship, the *Explorer of the Sea*, is headed for the Caribbean. We boarded yesterday, part of the Tottenville High School Class of '56 alumni celebration. I thank God for MaryAnn (Palmer) Popper's invitation one year ago, since neither Tom nor I graduated in that class. The timing was perfect. Tom and I needed to get away from the most stressful four months of our lives. Our nine-year-old grandson, Thomas Paul Monahan V, was killed in their home fire December 17, 2007.

I was awakened around eleven o'clock at night on December 16 by my husband, who said Sharin called to say Tommy's house was on fire. We flew over there, having to park a block away due to all the fire engines on their block. The house, by then, was engulfed in smoke. All the windows were broken and crawling with firemen. We approached the front of the house in terror, asking where our family was. The front doors were open wide, and we could see that the front staircase was burned away. We may have stood there for only three minutes, but it seemed like an eternity. Finally, a fireman came over to tell us that one man was taken to Staten Island Hospital North and a little boy was taken to Staten Island Hospital South.

It turned out the man sent to Staten Island Hospital North was Bobby Ryan, who lives in the house across the street. He was on the phone with Tommy's sister, Ashley, who was in her college dorm at the time. He saw the flames from his house. He told Ashley what he saw and rushed across the street. He injured his arm severely when he broke a window in an attempt to rescue Tommy's family. Bobby was an important person in Tommy's life; Tommy loved him like an older brother.

The events leading up to this horrific moment are earth-shattering. My hand trembles as I write these words. Our son, Tom, was initially told that the children were out of the burning house. When Maria asked him where Gabrielle was, he screamed her name as he ran up the burning staircase in his bare feet. Halfway up the stairs, he saw Gabrielle standing in her bedroom doorway with her arms outstretched and her face frozen with fear. He grabbed her in his arms, staying close to the stairway wall, leading her out through the fire. When he brought her out of the house, he learned that Tommy was nowhere to be found. Everyone believed he had gone back into the house to rescue his dog, Sophie. Tom immediately went up to Tommy's bedroom window using his own house ladder. He screamed for his son to come to the window. Tom broke the window, giving the fire in the hallway an exit out of the house. He was overcome with the smoke that barreled out of the window. It singed his hair, including his nose hairs. He was in direct line of the fire; ten feet from the bedroom door.

A fireman had a fire department ladder in hand. He attempted to loosen the rope in order to extend that ladder higher. Our son, Craig, a recently retired fireman who lives on the block, came running over to help. He jumped on the fireman's ladder to get to the bedroom as quickly as possible. At the same time, other firemen had water on the fire through the front door. Since Tom had ventilated the house, Craig was able to search Tommy's bedroom. However, due to the smoke and lack of oxygen, Craig was unable to get out of the bedroom and into the hallway. A fireman with an oxygen mask found Tommy on his sister's bedroom floor. Coincidently, the fireman who found and carried Tommy out of the house was a distant cousin that he had never met. Both Craig and Tom went in the ambulance with Tommy to the hospital.

We are so grateful that our son, Tom, was able to reach Gabrielle and save her life. Though he suffered smoke inhalation and singed hair and required stitches in his leg, he refused medical attention until we were ready to leave the hospital to go home. The only reason he finally went back to the emergency room was because he needed to be well for Gabrielle.

I couldn't believe that only twelve hours earlier, I had taken our granddaughters to visit an elderly shut-in to give her a Christmas book and listen to her Christmas memories. The girls took turns reading *A Christmas Cup of Tea* to her and sang "Silent Night" before leaving. No one was prepared to end this day in such pain. God help us!

We flew to the hospital following a police escort and were immediately ushered into the emergency room to find the most horrific scene. Our two sons, Craig and Tom, were in their nightclothes in a terrified state, standing close to Tommy's stretcher. Tom told the doctors to let me be at little Tommy's side. Our beautiful baby boy was lying on a stretcher. The clothes that had been cut off him were lying on the floor of the emergency room. He was hooked up to oxygen, and the diligent nurses and doctors were working on him. Paramedics had lost him at the house, but they managed to resuscitate him.

As I approached, I talked softly, yet clearly, to him. "Tommy, Grandma and Grandpa are here with you right now. We are with Dad and Uncle Craig. We will not leave you for a minute. We know you must be frightened, but we are convinced you are in excellent hands and we will make sure you get everything you need. I love you so much, and I am so proud of who you are. I will never leave your side, no matter what." One side of his face was burned, and a few spots on his forehead and hair were singed. The burns looked more like sunburn than a fire burn. It didn't appear as though he had been in contact with the flames. I continued, "Tommy, I want you to feel all the healing energy that surrounds you. The energy is so peaceful and serene. As you breathe in, feel the healing energy come into your body and blow out all the crap that is inside you."

Standing at his head, I stroked his hair and wiped the black liquid oozing from his nose and mouth at the same time. I commended him, "That's great, Tommy, you're doing your job. The crap is coming out; it's so healthy. Way to go." I kept reminding him who was there. "Dad, Grandpa, and Uncle Craig are still with us. I love you so much. All the angels and saints are also here to protect and keep you safe. I love you so much." He could also hear his dad's, Uncle Craig's, and Grandpa's voices. I talked to him nonstop, even when they had to start up his heart again and made me step behind the curtain. I called out to him, "Tommy, we are still here; you can't see us, but we are still here. We love you!"

The nurse, Victoria Novaro McLaughlin, was our ever-faithful savior. Although she only works part-time, she was always there when we needed to go to the emergency room. I had to calm my sons Tom and Craig down when little Tommy's heart stopped. Our son Tom's guttural, wrenching cries as he doubled over in pain were so difficult to hear. I had to remind him, "Tommy can hear you. We all need to remain in control for little Tommy's sake. I'm sorry I have to say this, Tom, but we can't let Tommy hear us out of control. We must keep focused on Tommy's needs right now."

My son Tom hugged me saying, "I know you're right, Mom, I know you're right."

The hospital sent little Tommy to Staten Island Hospital North by ambulance to the pediatric burn center. The doctor in charge at Staten Island Hospital South went along in the ambulance. The paramedics said no to my going in the ambulance, but the doctor said yes. That consoled me, as Victoria said, "Mrs. Monahan, you are great with little Tommy. Good luck; I will keep you all in my prayers." The police had every side street along Hylan Boulevard blocked off and escorted our ambulance from one hospital to the next. I sat up front with the driver, and Craig jumped into the back of the ambulance as they were closing the doors. The doctor allowed him to sit next to Tommy. Tom was already in Grandpa's car headed to the burn center. There was an entourage of doctors waiting for us. Initially they told me, my husband, Craig, and Tom to leave the room, until the doctor who escorted us told them we could stay.

From the moment I first saw Tommy that night through one and a half hours following his death, I was at his side talking to him. Our sons Tom and Craig were always close to him, rooting him on with words of encouragement and love. Grandpa was standing close by in prayer. Maria and Gabrielle had also arrived at the burn center by ambulance. I was aware the moment the doctors lost Tommy for the last time, but it seemed to me that the doctor in charge allowed the nurses and doctors to continue their efforts to save him for an extended period of time. The doctor in charge finally announced, "Note the time of death."

When those fatal words were spoken, our son Tom yelled, "*No,*" pushed the doctor aside, and proceeded to do CPR.

I attempted to take his hands away, pleading, "Let him go; he's at peace. Don't disturb him anymore."

Tom responded, "The heart monitor was registering activity."

I had to tell him that was from his compressions. "He's in the arms of the angels, saints, Grandpa Sal, and his great grandparents. He was without oxygen for too long to recover. If you revive him now, he will be brain dead."

With the life so physically drained from his body, my son Tom hugged his son, telling him how much he loved him and that he would always be with him.

Craig had been out of the room at the moment Tommy was pronounced dead. Shortly thereafter, when he returned, Craig also yelled, "*No,*" and attempted to do CPR.

I grabbed his hands, and his brother Tom told him to stop. "Craig, you wouldn't want Tommy to come back at this point."

Craig hugged little Tommy, with heartbroken tears flowing down his face. "I love you, Tommy, and I am so sorry I couldn't save you. I know you are with Blackie; please take care of him." Craig's dog Blackie had disappeared one year prior to this date.

Maria's cousins, Donna and Caryl, daughter Ashley, and mother Gloria arrived shortly thereafter. While the doctors at the burn center were working on my grandson Tommy, Grandpa had asked the nurses to call a priest. Father John from Holy Rosary came and was very comforting to us all. Our daughter Terry had also arrived and was at Tommy's bedside, talking with him constantly, reassuring him of her love for him.

Tears from each of us were unending. The pain and holes in our hearts continue to exist. How do we go on?

Maria and Tom gave permission to use Tommy's organs. Tom had to spend twenty minutes on the phone answering questions from the donor program, torn at not being able to be with Maria and Gabrielle at that time. My son Tom was furious when he was asked if his son Tommy had AIDS or had had sex with an AIDS carrier or if he was an IV drug user. Unfortunately, those questions are necessary; but in a moment like that, you can't help but feel hurt and angry to be asked such things. The hospital staff was extremely supportive and allowed us to stay with my grandson Tommy as long as we needed to, until they had to take him for the organs.

It turned out, that never happened. He had inhaled too much smoke and they had injected so many drugs into his heart, they could not use his organs. We did not know that until the next day. On this day, the hospital administration continued to come to me when they saw I was trying to keep everyone under control. It was then that I realized I was going to have to take on that role with this family. I needed to keep my emotions under control so clear decisions that needed to be made could be made appropriately.

Those moments were the worst moments of all our lives. We will never be the same. My only consolation is that I was sure the Blessed Mother was with Tommy from the moment he felt fear of what was happening. I pleaded with her from the moment I was awakened by the news of the fire and said the "Hail Mary" repeatedly from that moment on. Tommy's face, from the first moment I saw him through the one and a half hours following his death, never looked stressed, fearful, or pained. Only the Blessed Mother or the Lord has that much power. I prayed constantly, relying on the Blessed Mother, Jesus, and the Holy Spirit to guide my choices, actions, and words.

We needed to leave the hospital. We were grateful Tom and Maria wanted to go home with us. Terry came to help me clear out the big bedroom upstairs. It was filled with Christmas decorations, boxes, and all our Christmas gifts. The next day, I cleaned out all the dresser drawers, making room for the new belongings people were bringing the family to replace their lost or damaged things. It was about 4:30 a.m. when everyone went to bed. No one could sleep, but they went to try and rest. I sat at the kitchen table to pray the rosary and ask God to give me the strength to guide and take care of our family. In the midst of the rosary, I remembered an experience I had three days prior. It actually started one and a half weeks ago when I was at the Little Shop of Angels.

CHAPTER 2:
Premonitions

"I will call to the Lord for help; I plead with Him."
(Psalms 142:1)

As a bereavement minister, I had attended the wake of a ten-year-old boy who had died as a result of a seizure disorder. Seeing his mom curled up on the funeral parlor chair, with a woman coddling her, was heartbreaking. He had three sisters and a dad who was greeting people in the funeral home. The father was grateful for my outreach as I handed him lots of pamphlets and a brochure of our parish program to help grieving families.

As a rule, I only attend the funerals of people I know, but I was driven to attend this child's funeral. I did so and was overcome with sadness throughout the Mass, asking God to show me how to comfort the family. I prayed to the little boy to help me know how to reach his mom and sisters. After the Mass, not knowing anyone there, I felt the urge to drive to the Little Shop of Angels in the hope of finding a way to help this family.

I parked the car down the street, and as I approached the store, I noticed a man smoking a cigarette out front. I nodded good morning to him, and he did the same to me. I entered the store to be greeted by my friend, the owner, Lisa. She hugged and kissed me asking how I was. Trembling and tearful, I said, "I'm so disturbed by the funeral I just came from."

With that, the man entered the store. Lisa proceeded to say, "Oh Pat, I want you to meet Ed; and Ed, you need to meet Pat."

Ed immediately asked, "Do you know a little boy about so high?" (He demonstrated the height with his hand.) He described the boy's appearance; "He's slender with chubby cheeks and very short, sandy-brown hair."

My immediate reaction, though I didn't say it, was, *That's my grandson Tommy.* I asked him, "Do you mean he's of the spirit world?"

He said, "Yes, this boy followed you up the street and into the store and he was dancing around you. He needed you to know he was happy in heaven."

My response was, "Oh my God. That has to be the boy whose funeral I just came from. I prayed to him for a way to help his family. I'll have to find a way to pass on this message."

Ed went to the back of the store, returning with the book *Just a Breath Away*, the story he had written of his life's journey as a gifted medium. He autographed the book and handed it to me. He then proceeded to the back of the store with the woman who had just entered. He was to do a reading for her. I was so affected by this experience I made an appointment to have a reading with him. That reading took place the Friday prior to the fire.

During the reading, Ed saw the Blessed Mother with me. She reached into her heart, holding the sacred heart in two hands, and was giving it to me. He saw my mother worried about my heart, my father tapping his wrist with two fingers over and over, and Father Mychal Judge patting my son Craig on the shoulder telling him everything would be okay. Ed told me my son Tom was leaning heavily on me and calling, "Mom, Mom, Mom."

He asked me if I'd ever been in a big fire; and when I said no, he asked what fire meant to me. I could only think it was connected to Craig, since he was a fireman. Craig had experienced the tragic death of Captain John Drennan at the Watt Street fire ten years earlier; had been present at the World Trade Center on 9/11, when they lost eleven men and his friend, Father Judge; and most recently, had suffered the deaths of two friends in the tragic Deutsche Building fire. The only other option for the meaning of fire was the flame of the Holy Spirit. I pray to the Holy Spirit continually for guidance.

Ed then told me my husband had a heart problem. I told him he didn't. However, in March, my husband Tom had a heart attack and a stent was put in his heart. It didn't surprise me, since all our hearts were broken.

When asked by Ed, "Do you have any questions for me?" I asked, "Is someone close to me going to die?" I had recently had an instinct that my husband or I was going to die.

As soon as the question came out of my mouth, Ed anxiously began blowing over his right shoulder and then his left shoulder, over and over again. He responded frantically, "Don't think about death! Only think positive, not negative. Get death thoughts out of your mind." He told me, "We will all die someday. That's the order of life, but you must not think death."

At the kitchen table that fatal Monday morning after Tommy's passing, as I was saying the rosary, I realized Ed saw my grandson, Tommy, not the little boy who had died of the seizure disorder. His reading was all related to our fatal fire. I was sobbing from guilt. I should have known what was going to happen from his messages. I pleaded with God, "Please, please help me with this guilt." I called upon all the angels, the saints, and my parents to help me. Then I experienced a wave of peace rush from my head down through my body telling me, "There was no way you could have known that. You were not powerful enough to stop what happened."

I began to see these experiences as a reassurance that the Blessed Mother, my parents, and Father Judge were there, helping us through this tragedy, and that our beloved Tommy *was* happy in heaven. How grateful I was that he came to me with that message. I thanked "all the above from heaven" for the blessings bestowed on us at this worst time of our lives. When I told Tommy and Maria about my new awareness, they, too, believed it was a good message and weren't angry I couldn't piece the reading together to stop the fire or Tommy's death.

There had been so many signs as we look back these past months that God was preparing us for this inevitable loss. A few months prior, Tommy was at our house while my husband and I were at the kitchen table. Tommy spotted a coin on the table and picked it up to ask Grandpa where this angel coin came from and how much it was worth. Grandpa and Tommy always talked about their coins. It was a shared hobby, and Grandpa often gave Tommy the quarters he was looking for.

That day Grandpa told him the coin came in the mail from a religious charity to which we had donated.

Tommy took the gold coin off the table, examined both sides, which each had an angel on them, and asked Grandpa, "Grandpa, is this a free pass to heaven?"

Grandpa said, "You got it, Tommy." Tommy had that coin with his collection when he died, and Grandpa put it in the palm of his hand, under his cousin Joey's soccer glove, as he lay in his tiny coffin.

The last month of his life, Tommy and his sister Gabrielle were taking turns sleeping in each other's rooms. She started by asking him, "Tommy, can I sleep in your other bed?"

That night he said, "Yes, Gabrielle, but only if you pay me one dollar." She did. The next night he told his mom she could sleep there and not have to give him money (after having been chastised by his mom for making his sister give him money).

My guess is their souls anticipated their upcoming separation and they needed to sleep in the same room that last month to prepare for his leaving.

Tommy never liked hugs and kisses; but the last six months of his life, he not only allowed me to hug and kiss him, but he hugged me back. At the time, I commented to my husband how grateful I was that I received this gift from him.

Now I truly treasure those memories.

Immersed in Earth Camp

CHAPTER 3:
The Morning After

"The Lord is near the brokenhearted and
saves the crushed in spirits."
(Psalms 34:18)

At five o'clock in the morning, I wanted to call our parish office to ask them to start praying for Tommy at the daily Masses, beginning at 7:00 a.m. I could only get through to an answering machine. At six thirty I called Mary and Richard Ginocchio, requesting they go to the 7:00 a.m. Mass to speak with a priest. I couldn't leave the house because we were expecting a call from the medical examiner's office, and I didn't want the phone to wake anyone up if they were sleeping.

Thankfully our son Kevin and his wife, Linda, showed up. First, it was so good to get hugs from two more of our children. Second, Kevin said he'd stay by the phone so Linda and I could go to Mass. It was so comforting to be in church and receive the Holy Eucharist only hours after our little one's soul entered the kingdom of heaven. I was also grateful that Linda was with me. Mary and Richie were there, along with other parishioners offering their help and hugs. Mary gave me a composition notebook to keep by the phone to help us record the visits and offerings people would be bringing. That book was a godsend, a most meaningful gesture.

When we returned from Mass, Craig came over, filled with emotion about an experience he had that morning. Upon returning from the hospital, he went to my son Tom's house to put a two-by-four wooden plate on the floor in order to secure the temporary stairs he was going to build that morning. He wanted the family to be able to see if anything upstairs could be salvaged. While kneeling on the floor with his back to the front door, he felt heat on his back. As he turned toward the door, he saw a white light rushing from the door to the spot on the floor where the fire began. The room was illuminated with the light, and he saw the Blessed Mother standing there with Tommy in her arms. She told him that we were supposed to "Tell everybody to pray the rosary for Tommy, even if they don't know how or don't believe in it." The message was so powerful and the vision so clear and beautiful he believed he had to pay attention, so he ran over immediately to tell us.

When the medical examiner's office called requesting someone from the family to come to identify the body, I asked Tom and Maria if I could go. I had promised Tommy I'd be there for him every step of the way. My son Scott insisted on going with me. When we arrived at the facility, the waiting room was empty. I felt the blood leave my body as we walked in, but I was glad I was there and very grateful that Scott was with me. He's got a peaceful and prayerful aura about him. His inner strength gave me comfort and security. We stood at the front desk in silence. All of a sudden, a cat jumped up in front of us from behind the counter. As startled as we were, this cat turned out to be peaceful and comforting as it rubbed back and forth along my arm, which was resting on the counter. It brought tears to my eyes as I responded to the cat. I knew Tommy's spirit was with him. I told Tommy, "I am fulfilling my promise to you, and I am so grateful you met Uncle Scott and me here." I spoke to the cat, acknowledging him as I said, "Thank you for being here for Tommy. Have fun together while Tommy is here."

I had forgotten my identification (necessary for the viewing); but while I was talking with the cat, Scott found someone to help with the process so I could be the one to identify Tommy. Scott and I were called into a small room, and the staff was extremely sensitive. We only had to identify the picture they took of Tommy at the medical examiner's facility. Praise the Lord, he looked like he was sleeping peacefully. We were filled with gratitude.

CHAPTER 4:
The Wake and Funeral

"God, be merciful to us and bless us; look on us with kindness."
(Psalms 67:1)

O ur family, neighbors, and friends were there for us in every way. People were there for us with morning coffee, breakfast, lunches, dinners, snacks, and fruit baskets. Clothes for everyone were here before Tom and Maria knew they needed to change their clothes. Gabrielle's needs were anticipated and responded to by more people than we could count. Paul Pizzo and his sister Barbara from Bedell Funeral Home could not have been more sensitive and generous to our needs as we made plans for Tommy's last days on this Earth. Paul informed us that other funeral directors had also called to offer their help. Hall Monuments generously fulfilled our every need to bury Tommy in the most memorable way—so any stranger passing by would see what a special boy he was and what he was all about. Betsy Hall Mahoney did a magnificent job designing the stone.

The wake was quite emotional, but very comforting to all of us. This experience, as painful as it was, helped us all appreciate the significance of the Catholic ritual of a wake. Initially, Maria thought she could only handle a one-day wake.

I told her, "Be prepared! That single day will be very difficult. We know the number of people who would want to show up. It will be overwhelming, and most of them would not get in due to the time constraints." I also advised, "You need to accept that you will have to see these people at some time; which might prove to be more difficult.

In the funeral home, the structure allows for an easier greeting. In the funeral home, you expect people will be there. A casual encounter on the street or in a store could be more uncomfortable."

It was decided we would have a two-day wake, with the understanding that Tom and Maria could leave anytime they felt they couldn't handle it. As difficult as the wake was, it was also comforting. Maria and Tom were so grateful we had the two days. The number of people who came to show their respect was overwhelming. The line of visitors went out the door and down the street. What amazed us were the politicians! They chose to wait in the long line like everyone else. The respect shown was quite humbling. My husband, a fourth-degree member of the Knights of Columbus and a member of the K. of C. Color Corps, was so touched by the representation of his brother knights. They came to pray and, at the same time, to pay their respects to our family as a group. There was barely enough room for all of them to stand together in prayer. In fifty years of Knights of Columbus membership, my husband never saw such a large turnout of brother knights at any wake, especially when the deceased was only a family member of a knight, not a knight himself. The American Legion was another surprise. It is also their custom to only attend the wake of another veteran, yet they all came in uniform to demonstrate their support.

And the children—our hearts went out to *all* the children. My primary concern was for Gabrielle. At eight years of age, she should not be saying good-bye to the brother she loved so much. Everyone knew how much they loved each other. It warmed my soul whenever I saw them express their love for the other. Fighting often, as all siblings do, especially when so close in age and opposite sexes, they looked out for each other always. If you gave one of them something, such as a homemade brownie, they'd request one for their sibling. If one of them was hurt, they would try and soothe the hurt. So many of the things Tommy loved went to heaven with him.

Gabrielle wanted to send her stuffed lizard with him because Tommy always wanted to play with it. Uncle Scott had to search the debris of the fire for the lizard. He engaged others at the house to help. It was found, eventually, soaked and filthy from the fire. Scott rushed it to the local dry cleaner in the hope that they could have it prepared for that afternoon's wake. When they heard it was for the boy who lost his life in the fire, they rushed it through and wouldn't accept payment. It was slightly damp but ready just in time for Tommy's viewing that first afternoon. I am so grateful to God that Gabrielle feels her brother around her and mentions signs of his presence. He will clearly never leave her, and she will never forget him.

I knew I was going to be the one to give Tommy's eulogy. So I prayed hard, asking for guidance on what to say. After much prayer, the words just flowed out onto the paper. One thing I knew for sure was that I was going to ask everyone to pray the rosary for Tommy and would be happy to tell them how if they didn't know. Our church, Saint Joseph–Saint Thomas in Pleasant Plains, was packed. The Ancient Order of Hibernians' Honor Guard lined the entrance to the church as the bagpipers played. We were so honored, since their protocol is to only show up for their deceased members. There was standing room only in the church.

We were pleasantly surprised to see twelve apostles on the altar. Monsignor Tom Modugno from Saint Monica's (the co-vicar of Manhattan) was there, as were Monsignor Peter Finn, pastor of Blessed Sacrament Church (co-vicar of Staten Island); our pastor, Monsignor Edmond Whalen; Father John Palatucci and Father Gil from our church; Father Pros from Our Lady Help of Christians; Father Kevin Malick from St. Augustin's; Father Michael Martine of St. Joseph's Seminary; Father Steve Ryan from Our Lady of the Valley in Orange, New Jersey; Father Michael Cichon, pastor of the Church of the Assumption and St. Paul; Father Joe Roesch, a Marian priest in Rome; and Deacon Artie Fama, of St. Anthony's of Padua, Red Bank, New Jersey. Monsignor Finn said this was the first time there were so many priests on the altar at the same time in this church. We were so blessed and honored.

The Mass was the most beautiful Mass possible as far as funerals go. Everyone said they felt an overwhelming sense of love and peace in the church. It clearly was a celebration of Tommy's life. God was so good to us. We are forever grateful to all who came to honor Tommy's life and help all of us to send him back home to the Lord. We are so grateful to God for sharing Tommy with us for his nine years on Earth. We were overwhelmed with grief, but at the same time, overwhelmed with gratitude for everyone's attendance, support, and prayers, as well as the message that Tommy was happy in heaven. The funeral entourage received a police escort, and the procession of cars extended a few miles. The Ancient Order of Hibernians' Bagpipers accompanied us to the cemetery as well.

Maria and Tom arranged to have two white doves released at the cemetery at the close of the service, one for Tommy and one for Sophie. The lid of the bird carrier was lifted to release the doves, but they never flew away. It was amazing. Everyone believed they didn't want to leave Tommy. The doves looked at each other and just hung out. I could see Tommy laughing. Eventually the owner had to coax them to fly away. It was beautiful, but not surprising. We know Tommy's spirit flies freely in the sky.

As we approached the final resting place, the weather was inclement. There was a gray, misty hue in the air, and we hoped it wouldn't start raining. Our emotions fit the cold air. It was a most depressive moment. The only sound to be heard was the cooing from the doves.

Almost magically, the moment the doves flew away, the sun began to shine, the air warmed, and the atmosphere, both physically and emotionally, was infused with a sense of peace. My grandson Joey shot a startled look to his mother. She nodded to him, acknowledging what he was experiencing. When Gabrielle, Joey, and Aunt Terry (Joey's mom) returned to the car, the conversation persisted. Joey said, "I was freezing, and the sky was so dark and cloudy. It was like a miracle! As soon as the doves flew away, the sun came out, and I was warmed to my bones."

Gabrielle said, "Me too!"

Joey continued, "I know it was Tommy. Now I know he went to heaven."

Tommy's magnificent tombstone was put in place in May. It's such a tribute to who he was (and always will be to all who know and love him.) The stone depicts Tommy as the angel in front of St. Francis. The collar of his soccer jersey can be seen from under his robe. Sophie is on Tommy's lap and they are surrounded by some of Tommy's animal friends. Spohie's name is under the paw print in the upper right hand corner of the stone. There is a plant enclosure attached to the stone. An engraved arrowhead is on one side of the planter and a soccer ball is on the other side.

When Uncle Craig and cousins Craigie and Christian saw the stone for the first time, the two boys placed two toy snakes on the grave, and

Uncle Craig was overwhelmed with grief. We all cry a lot over this beautiful boy we all loved more than words can say.

Tommy's final resting place

CHAPTER 5:
First Steps Forward

"Those who sow in tears shall reap rejoicing."
(Psalms 126:5)

That first week was a blur. We don't know what we would have done without our friends, neighbors, and the entire community. The earthly angels surrounded us. Visitors bearing food and clothes and the phone calls and visits were so comforting. We were overwhelmed with all the love and support beyond belief. Everyone shared our pain and tears. We were filled with their love.

Our church gave the family the use of a house that was in move-in condition. Friends and strangers called to offer their empty houses for as long as was needed. House builders offered to find a house our family could use anywhere on Staten Island.

God's presence was obvious through the people that came out in droves to respond to our family's crisis. The fire marshals and insurance company finished their investigation. Apparently the cause of the fire was aged, defective wiring in the basement ceiling under the main staircase. Without delay, families, neighbors, friends, and strangers converged on the property prepared to tackle whatever job was necessary to empty the house of salvageable items and to gut the interior. Craig's brother firemen from Ladder 5/Engine 24, Greenwich Village, came as a unit.

Every day there was a minimum of thirty people energetically performing their tasks. Sometimes there were up to sixty people at one time, from early in the morning until dark. Dumpsters were ordered and delivered in an inordinately short period of time. It wasn't uncommon to see a pizza delivery truck pull up with twenty free pies and soda. Hero sandwiches and cases of cold drinks were unexpectedly dropped off. Dozens and dozens of donuts and gallons of coffee appeared on the spot. It was reminiscent of an old-fashioned barn raising. Volunteers converged together with a common purpose.

Who Says There Is No God?

I was also blessed one day weeks after the funeral. While swimming at the YMCA, I was approached by a strange woman. We never saw each other before, but she claimed she saw the Blessed Mother watching over me while I was swimming and said the Blessed Mother told her to tell me she is always with me. The woman did not know who I was but told me she was directed to give me this information. God is good.

CHAPTER 6:
Signs of Tommy

"Love never gives up: and its faith, hope, and
patience never fails. Love is eternal."
(1 Corinthians 13:7–8)

On Friday, April 18, while sitting on the ship's deck after having prayed my daily rosary, looking at the gorgeous, blue sea with the pale-blue sky overhead filled with small, white, puffy clouds, I was grateful for God's blessings and getting through the four-month anniversary of Tommy's death with such evidence of God's love and presence of our grandson.

Elinor Hutchinson (Tottenville High School Class of '56) was on board with our group, and yesterday was the first anniversary of her beloved husband, Tom's, death. I had offered to help her acknowledge that day. She requested we say the rosary, and we planned to do so in the ship's chapel at eight o'clock in the morning, the same time his anniversary Mass was being said back home in Tom's River. I put a little prayer service together, and approximately eighteen people attended our service and joined us in the rosary. Elinor had a picture of Tom and shared stories about his life. I gave her a candle from the ceremony to take home with her. The service was very meaningful and helpful to all who attended.

That afternoon as my husband, Tom, arose from a nap, I found two dimes that had fallen out of his pocket. They were a clear sign to us that Tommy was saying hi. For the bereaved, finding unexplainable coins is a clear sign the deceased are communicating with us. Compassionate

Friends, a support group for parents who have lost children, believes dimes are what the children leave. Coming through another *dime*nsion, the children leave the smallest coin.

Following Grandpa Tom's nap, we got ready for dinner. Approaching the dining room, I was stopped by a classmate (Lynn Hayden Ellis), who told me her spiritualist friend, who was traveling with them and seated at her table, told her a young spirit was with me and dancing around me needing me to know he was happy in heaven and I should not feel guilty; I could not have prevented his death. This was clearly another gift from God.

While ashore, Elinor went to the church in San Juan where Ponce de Leon is buried. He was an explorer. Tommy would have loved knowing him. Elinor came to my table before dinner to give me a beautiful white pair of delicate rosary beads she bought for me as a thank you for that day's ceremony.

The evidence of God's love and Tommy's presence this day was overwhelming. I am truly blessed, and I praise the Lord and thank all His messengers.

There have been so many signs of God's love and Tommy's presence. Despite the pain of losing our special grandson Tommy, I am so filled with God's graces and don't know what I would do without my faith. I cry a lot and try to remember to live each day as though it was my last, as we have always been told to do by our church. I truly understand the dynamics of that directive, and we are fortunate to have our faith to lead us.

Every Easter we have an egg hunt in our backyard. I fill approximately two hundred plastic eggs with small toys or coins. Easter morning Grandpa helps the Easter Bunny hide the eggs in the house and backyard. This year, Lent had a more personal significance to us. I could feel Saint Anne's pain in losing a grandchild. I'm not comparing Tommy's death with the Crucifixion; I'm only identifying with the pain of losing a grandson.

Since Tom and his family were still living with us, he and Gabrielle colored the Easter eggs and helped me fill the plastic eggs. While taking my collection of eggs out of the storage bin, Tom found an unopened army camouflaged egg with a toy soldier in it. Tom's eyes filled with tears, convinced his son was letting him know that he was with him.

Gabrielle found an unopened egg from last year with dimes in it. There are no coincidences. Tommy was with them that evening, and they both knew it. I took one of the army filled camouflaged eggs and a frog inside a toy frog bunny egg and placed them on Tommy's grave on Holy Saturday.

Three months after Tommy's death, my husband, Tom, was in the hospital recovering from a heart attack. He was wakened in the middle of the night and saw Tommy standing at his bedside smiling and looking peaceful. He walked up to Grandpa and gave him a big hug. Grandpa felt the hug as though Tommy was physically present. Grandpa remembered the last time he saw Tommy alive. Tommy was being picked up from our house by his mom to go for a haircut. Grandpa had given Tommy a big hug, kissed him on the forehead, and told him, "I love you, Tommy."

They clearly had a special relationship. Tommy loved seeing Grandpa. They talked about so many of their similar interests. He was proud that Grandpa was a navy captain and admired his captain's sword. Tommy loved going to see Grandpa and the American Legion veterans honor the deceased veterans at their memorial service each year. He stood by Grandpa, so proud as he saluted the American Flag. After the rifles were shot, he collected and saved the bullet shells. Grandpa had to go to the memorial service to honor the deceased vets without Tommy this year. He brought home a flag and a bullet shell to put on Tommy's grave on Memorial Day. Grandpa was tearful without Tommy at the ceremony, and Tommy was not forgotten by the other veterans either. He will *never* be forgotten.

Shortly after Tommy died, his mother, Maria, was struggling to see signs of him, since many of us were clear about his presence. On Valentine's Day, my friend Dolores gave me a small cactus plant while we were cofacilitating the Bereavement Support Group. We had given each of our group members a flower that evening. She had gone into the florist to buy me a flower but had difficulty choosing which flower to buy. She reported to me she couldn't understand why and thought it strange, but she found herself drawn to this little cactus plant with two green blossoms on it.

Maria was asleep when I brought it home and placed it on the kitchen counter. However, she was the first one to enter the kitchen in the morning. As I was leaving for the YMCA, she asked where the plant came from. She cried when I told her my gift bearer and story. She then believed the plant came from Tommy, and we concur. Three Christmases ago when asked what he wanted for Christmas, he said, "Toy soldiers and a cactus plant."

Tommy's parents, Tom and Maria, will never forget their birthdays this year. The Sunday preceding Tom's birthday, our church bulletin informed us that a Mass was being said for Tommy on his dad's birthday. I inquired at the parish office about who had this Mass said, but no name was given. We believe Tommy was responsible for inspiring that anonymous soul, and we gave prayers of thanks to God for them.

During that Mass, the lights in the church flickered. We all looked at each other because we believe the deceased have the energy to play games, and we were convinced Tommy wanted his dad to know he was present.

While we all sat at the breakfast table that morning, the small television on the kitchen counter spontaneously turned on. The television controls were not near anyone. Tommy wished his dad a happy birthday.

Early in the morning of Maria's birthday, when Maria was sitting at our kitchen table, two trains (each going in different directions) stopped behind our backyard, both blasting their horns. She knew immediately Tommy was wishing her a happy birthday. The trains pass by our house every half hour but never at the same time, and the only time they blow their horns is when someone is on the train tracks. No one was there that morning. That is, no one of this world.

On three separate occasions, when I awoke at six o'clock in the morning to go swimming at the YMCA, as I approached the dining room (attached to the kitchen), the kitchen television went on. Of course, I said good morning to Tommy, as is my routine upon awaking.

On Tommy's close friend Gavin's birthday, there was another electrical incident. Gavin was sitting at his dining room table doing his homework. He was alone in the room that overlooks Tommy's bedroom window. A light bulb in the overhead chandelier burst. Of course, it startled Gavin, but his mom affirmed that Tommy was saying happy birthday. What a comfort to a hurting friend.

Our son Craig came over one morning to show us a videotape he had made in his backyard. He and his boys see signs of Tommy in their yard all the time. One day, Craig decided to capture the moment for others to witness. Young Craig and Christian were in the house with him. From the kitchen window, he began taping two young squirrels playing with each other. Out of the corner of his eye, he detected movement on the swing set. He pointed his camera that way; and sure enough, the middle of the three swings was swaying back and forth, a scene he and the boys had often witnessed. All of a sudden as it swayed back and forth, one of the squirrels leaped up and onto the swing. He enjoyed riding the swing to and fro for a few moments before jumping down. What a sight to see, and how validating to the boys. They now had evidence Tommy is hanging out in their yard just as they thought. Young Craig said, "That was Tommy's favorite swing."

As I sit on my front porch writing at this moment, I can hear Tommy through the bird's songs and the freedom of the butterfly sitting on my porch flower. Signs of a thunderstorm are starting to appear. I guess he's reminding me he can make all the noise he wants to right now. I hear his laughter with the sounds of thunder. I see his spirit flying swiftly with the breeze as it spins my hanging plants, flaps around our American flag atop our flagpole, and rustles the trees. *I hear and see you, Tommy. I love you, no matter the form you take. You are forever in our hearts and minds.* There's peace in all God's creations, regardless of how dark the clouds get and how heavy the rain falls. His love is everlasting.

CHAPTER 7:
Tommy's Pond

*"Let the field be joyful, and all that is in it. Then all
the trees of the woods will rejoice before the Lord."*
(Psalms 96:12)

Our son Tom made arrangements with the New York City
Department of Environmental Protection to adopt a section
of Skunk's Pond on Scudder Avenue, Princess Bay, as a gift to
Maria for Mother's Day. Dad and Son went there often on their wildlife
excursions. This was the spot they placed the turtles they'd find.

It also happened to be a part of the pond that Grandpa and I called
"our place" from 1953 through 1957. We would end up there on our
daily walks, sit alone on a tree stump, and watch the turtles rear their
heads out of the water. We'd hope to be the one to see the first turtle.
The first gift Grandpa gave me when we were teenagers was three turtle
pins. I still have two of them. I pinned them onto one of the thank-you
cards we sent out to everyone; we placed it in front of Tommy's picture
on our buffet.

I remember my son Tom spending much of his childhood in the
woods. The Staten Island Railway runs two hundred feet beyond
our house, up on a hill. Tom often crossed those tracks to spend
hours wandering through the woods to Lemon Creek. In grammar
school, he trapped muskrats, skinned them, and sold their pelts, as
was commonplace in this neck of the woods. My grandson Tommy's
love of nature and all its creatures came from his dad, who thirsted
for knowledge of the history of Staten Island. Tommy's mom, Maria,

fostered his love of nature by spending time chauffeuring him to Lemon Creek and Earth Camp.

At nine o'clock Mother's Day morning, I walked to "Tommy's Pond" and sat on the wall to pray the rosary to the Blessed Mother to thank her for taking care of our Tommy. I knew as soon as I saw Tommy in the hospital that the Blessed Mother was with him. The medium Ed said she was with him and that Tommy had just fallen asleep and had never felt fear; I believed him. I just knew it from the look on Tommy's face. The Blessed Mother is the reason Tommy never felt fear. Remember that Craig saw the vision that Mary was carrying him peacefully in her arms. The Blessed Mother gives him hugs, and I'm so grateful to her.

Two turtles popped up while I was praying the rosary at the pond. I was so surprised because the neighbors had said that the Parks Department had removed many turtles from this pond. They questioned if there were any left. The larger of the two, the size of my palm, climbed onto a branch at the edge of the water, stretched his neck, and sat there until I finished the rosary. The little one swam away after being unsuccessful at climbing up. I was so grateful and talked to Tommy, knowing he was responsible for the turtles appearing. Days later, I walked there again to say the rosary, and I saw six turtles after I began my prayers. They had been on the opposite side of the pond and swam my way. I'm convinced Tommy sent them to me as a gift. I talked to him through my tears and gratitude. God is so good. I'm a grateful grandma.

On June 18, I took another walk to Tommy's Pond to see the work Tom, Chris Walsh, and two of Chris' friends had done clearing paths in the woods. We had lots of rain these past weeks, and everything was overgrown. Maria gave Tom "the Rolls Royce of weed whackers" for Father's Day. He went to use it at the pond, and when he arrived Chris was there with his friends. Tom was overjoyed. There are no coincidences. What are the odds Chris showed up when Tom was there? It was divine intervention. God is good! He is all over with His graces. We are so grateful. They did a magnificent job clearing new paths through the woods and giving us a broader view of the pond.

I prayed my rosary while being serenaded by the birds and God's creatures. The men cleared the stone wall, giving us space to sit on the wall without getting scratched by the overgrown branches. When I go there to say the rosary, I use the beads our oldest granddaughter Kaitlyn brought me back from the Blessed Mother's house in Turkey. I placed an old set of rosary beads in the tree next to the wall. Since they were made of plastic beads and cord, they would not rust or damage the tree. Who knows? Someone may use them. If not, at least I know there is a religious icon in the most precious spot on Staten Island.

Top - Dad and Tommy exploring the beach
Bottom - Hug with sister Gabrielle

CHAPTER 8:
Tommy's Way

*"Comfort your hearts and establish you
in every good word and work."*
(2 Thessalonians 2:17)

I t's amazing how Tommy lives on in so many ways. This little boy
has touched so many lives. On June 24, P.S. 36, the school Tommy
had attended, had a dedication ceremony in their newly renovated
courtyard in memory of him. The Citizens' Committee at P.S. 36
contacted the Deloitte Accounting Co., requesting they assist in this
major renovation project in memory of Tommy. This international
accounting firm closes their offices one day every year, and their
employees volunteer that day in a major community project. They
responded enthusiastically after hearing about Tommy.

Tom, Maria, Grandpa, and I stopped by to thank them for their
efforts as they put all their energies into the magnificent collage and
garden. Some of the employees went to volunteer at the animal shelter
at the same time. We were so touched by their generosity and dedication
to this project. The collage includes the picture of a redheaded boy,
Tommy.

June 24 was a beautiful sunny day. The two classes of the school
that participated were Tommy's class 4-236 and Gabrielle's class 3-257.
The principal, Ms. Bellafatto, officiated and allowed Tommy's classmate
and soccer friend Phillip Lefkowitz to bring out the flag and lead the
Pledge of Allegiance. Tommy played for two soccer leagues, Staten
Island United travel league and Catholic Youth Organization (CYO)

recreational soccer. Phillip still had Tommy's travel soccer number shaved on the back of his head from the Staten Island United soccer tournament. Phillip was one of two soccer players who gave Tommy an incentive to play as hard as he could. Tommy aspired to play like his cousin Joey and Phillip. Both boys are hard playing, competitive, and passionate for their sport. Our family was thrilled to see Phillip leading the flag ceremony.

The welcoming greeting was very meaningful and an emotional beginning to a beautiful ceremony. Tommy's classmates read the poetry they wrote in Tommy's memory and placed their handmade stepping-stones in the garden. One stone had Tommy's initials made out of colored tiles. Their designs and signatures were so personal and warmed our hearts. Gabrielle's class presented birdhouses they had painted for the garden. One of Tommy's friends painted his soccer team number, 72, on one of the roofs. Gabrielle painted hearts.

There was a huge yellow ribbon around one of the trees in the garden, and Ms. Bellafatto led the ceremony as Maria, Tom, and Gabrielle cut the ribbon. The courtyard is now called "Tommy's Way." The wall opposite the garden has a painting of Tommy in the center lying on the ground, drawing a picture of the huge old tree that is painted on the adjacent wall, next to the entrance of the school. The sign over the door welcomes everyone to P.S. 36. It is so cheerful and uplifting.

I made brownies for Tommy's and Gabrielle's classes as well as for the boys at Monsignor Farrell's High School, who spent an entire day cleaning up and turning over the dirt in the garden area of the school. The Huguenot Garden Center donated some of the garden supplies and tree planted in Tommy's memory.

CHAPTER 9:
Lemon Creek and the Animal Shelter

"Then the wolf shall be a guest of the lamb, the leopard shall lie down with the kid, and the calf and the young lion shall browse together with a little child to lead them."
(Isaiah 11:6)

Tommy's parents raised him and Gabrielle to treat the environment and wildlife with great respect. The four of them participated in community clean-up projects. Tommy loved animals, nature, the environment, Native Americans, birds and their feathers, soccer, coins, rocks, stones, archeological artifacts, stamps, toy soldiers, tanks, trucks, baseball cards, Pokemon cards, war movies, the nature, science and history channels, and fishing in both fresh and salt water. However, he did not like school—until the September before he died. Those three months, he looked forward to school and loved his teacher. He didn't have a problem with doing his homework, especially in religion. This was the first year he had no problem learning his prayers, and the teacher and students report he was always raising his hand. I do believe he was preparing to leave this world as we know it.

Maria and Tom received a letter from a couple who are Native Americans and live on a reservation. Upon hearing about Tommy's love of the American Indian, they prayed for him on December 17 and sent copies of their prayers to the wings of the Eagle Spirit of the East, South, West, and North; Father Sky; and Mother Earth. They smoked the peace pipe in their sweat lodge and reported one of the elders of the tribe said, "Even at nine, Tommy was enlightened."

The Parks Department on Staten Island knew Tommy very well. They met him on his excursions to Lemon Creek, where he'd save the horseshoe crabs. They knew he was taking care of the environment, so they let him in some restricted areas. The horseshoe crabs would come in with the high tide and get caught among the rocks in a small tidal pool the residents called a lagoon. Tommy knew how to hold them, gently pick the parasites off their underbelly, scrape the barnacles off their backs with a seashell, and gently return them to the water. The park rangers knew him so well they made him an honorary park ranger once they witnessed his knowledge of and sensitivity with all of nature's creatures. He was the neighborhood "snake expert." Everyone knew to call him if they found a snake in their yards. Always rescuing snapping turtles, he'd bring them to their natural habitat where they'd be safe.

Tommy's preschool teacher never experienced a child like him. He was the one young boy who found a snapping turtle in the woods behind the school. He didn't play on the swings in the miniplayground. He was always off in the woods.

When Tommy was in grade school his teacher and classmates screamed out loud when they found a centipede in school. They didn't know what kind of bug it was. Tommy jumped out of his seat, slid on the floor, gently picked up the bug, and released it outside the school. Tommy rescued a praying mantis from Patty Monreale's hair since she was fearful of bugs. Patty once asked Tommy to take a bug off her window box so she could water her plants. He told her it was only a dragonfly that wouldn't hurt her.

Tommy was upset one day getting off the school bus. His substitute teacher for the day left the science department's delivery of anoles in boxes. She knew nothing about anoles and didn't unwrap them. He was so afraid they wouldn't have enough oxygen and food to live through the weekend. He took flyers from the pet store to the school to educate the teachers and students how to effectively care for anoles. There are numerous stories like these about Tommy's compassion.

His mom and dad reflected on the day after they took down the Halloween and Thanksgiving decorations in the front and back of their house. They had stacked the Indian corn, preparing it for the garbage. Tommy scraped the corn from the cob to put some into the large seashell he had and some into his lizard's old water dish. He placed them in two different sections of the yard to feed the birds. The largest poster in his bedroom was a Native American chief, because he loved and respected Mother Earth.

Uncle Craig was so grateful he took Tommy along with his sons, Craig and Christian, on their nature excursions. His fondest memory was last summer when he took Tommy and Craig through Acme Woods to go fishing before sunrise. Young Craig (then four years old) jumped out of bed when Dad woke him for their fishing trip with Tommy. Uncle Craig said they had to get there before the fish woke up because that's when they're hungry. It was five o'clock in the morning, and Tommy was waiting at his back door, fishing pole in hand. The woods were pitch-black as they walked the Indian trails. Along the path, there was complete silence and peace. All of a sudden, they heard the rustling of a large bird's wings. A gigantic white owl with a six-foot wingspan flew up right in front of them. The boys were in their glory: a magnificent sight and an experience to last a lifetime. They didn't catch any fish that day and cried when they had to leave the pond, but they went home with joy in their hearts knowing that no one else they knew could say they had seen a white owl fly so close to them.

Tommy loved coming to our house. He would dart right out to the backyard with Grandpa searching for salamanders, snakes, worms, crickets, and any other creature to observe. They would look for wild animal tracks and feed the birds. They would pick Grandpa's grapes, figs, and vegetables. They searched through Grandpa's coins and he loved Grandma's home-cooking, especially her Mickey Mouse pancakes or waffles with fruit. His favorite time with us was when his cousins came here for sleepovers.

Grandpa was so grateful he was home one day last summer when I was doing something with the younger granddaughters. Tommy asked Grandpa to take him to the clay banks at Mt. Loretto Beach. Tommy had gone there with Earth Camp, but his age group was too young to climb the steep clay bank. Of course, he and Grandpa painstakingly attacked that bank, at least eighty feet high, until they reached the top. Once on top, looking out over Raritan Bay and out of breath from their climb, Tommy said, "Grandpa, if anyone was afraid of heights, they'd sure be scared up here." He felt so proud he made it to the top. He was so adventurous and enthusiastic about each experience.

Senator Andrew Lanza's office is making arrangements for a bench to be placed at Lemon Creek in Tommy's name. The senator and his staff have been so supportive to our family. Their concern is evidence that "a small fish in a big pond" is deserving of attention. That same concern has been evident in borough president James Molinaro and his staff. Their outreach efforts to us have been overwhelming and much appreciated. His Honor initiated the renovation of the Animal Shelter in the name of Thomas P. Monahan V. This is the shelter to which Tommy donated his own money to help animals in need. He had a coffee can in his kitchen where he put his money after organizing backyard sales with his friends in the neighborhood, selling their old toys. One of the children suggested they split their earnings 50/50, but Tommy insisted the animals needed it more. Some of his birthday and other monetary gifts were also put in the can.

Almost everything in the family's house was destroyed in the fire. However, after the firemen knocked things over while putting out the fire, Tommy's coffee can was intact. The outside of the can burned, but the plastic cover and money inside the can were undamaged. As a matter of fact, there was *one* cabinet containing Tommy's artwork that was untouched, even though everything surrounding that cabinet was severely damaged by water, smoke, and/or fire. The Lord works in strange ways. The effects of that coffee can went a long way. We cannot imagine how many animals have been saved as a result of Tommy and his coffee can.

On June 26, 2008, a bronze plaque honoring Tommy was unveiled by Borough President Molinaro at the new Thomas P. Monahan V Surgical Suite. His Honor funded this facility through his capital budget.

Earlier in the year, President Molinaro's office invited Tom, Maria, and the family to come to his office to discuss their plans for the animal shelter. During conversations about Tommy's visit to the Nature Conservancy to see Atka, the gray wolf, Lillian Lagasso, executive assistant to the borough president, asked the date of their visit. She then reached into her pocket, took out her cell phone, searched through her phone, and showed everyone pictures of Tommy and Atka on her cell phone. Lillian had taken a picture of the wolf as he was coming through the aisle of spectators. At that same moment, Tommy, close to the back of the audience, poked his head into the aisle. The picture clearly showed Tommy and the wolf. It turns out that while walking the aisle at the end of a strong leash, Atka stopped and sniffed Tommy, which is a rare occurrence. The date was March 25, 2007. What are the odds of someone keeping those pictures in their camera all those months? She had never met Tommy.

Duly elected members of the New York City Council recognized Tommy Monahan posthumously. They honored him "as an outstanding citizen, one which is worthy of the esteem of both the community and the great City of New York." This award was presented to our son Tom and his wife Maria by Councilman Michael McMahon. Charlene Pedrolie, executive director of Animal Care and Control, said, "Tommy Monahan lost his life trying to rescue the pets he loved. We were so pleased that Borough President Molinaro was honoring Tommy in such a special way. This is a fitting tribute because Tommy had such a deep concern for animals and often raised money to help care for the homeless pets in our shelter."

While filtering through the debris of the fire, Tommy's dad found the receipt of Tommy's last donation to the shelter. His parents knew then that they would request donations to an animal shelter in lieu of flowers. This shelter was overloaded with donations made in Tommy's name. We heard from shelters in other states, where benefits were also received in Tommy's name. A lawyer in New York City sent donations to a school in Massachusetts where his deceased mom had been the librarian. He specified his money should be spent on books related to Tommy's nature topics, with each book having a label with Tommy's name in it.

NYSAVE (New York Saves Animals in Veterinary Emergency) honored Tommy and Sophie as guardian angels to a New York City companion animal that needed veterinarian care. Sophie's name is in the pet heaven section at NYSAVE.

We were invited to the shelter at 10:30 a.m. on May 15 to welcome twelve students from the school's government body from P.S. 247, escorted by their teachers and the principal. They arrived by bus and brought with them bags and boxes of towels, blankets, toys, and food for the animals, as well as a check for $1,500.00 and a large collage painting of Tommy and the animals. They were making these donations in Tommy's memory. When questioned by the television interviewer why they came all the way from Bensonhurst, Brooklyn, to donate these items, their response was quite clear and simple: "We saw the television news about the boy who died in a house fire because he went back for his animals. We heard he was always saving his money to help the animals, and we wanted his memory to stay alive. We also hoped other people would do the same. It's the least we can do."

These children (in grades three through five) touched our souls to the core. We were all crying, but the tears were healing. Our son Tom told the children stories about Tommy and the animals through his tears, and they stood riveted to each and every word. When I showed them a picture of Tommy and a crab, Matthew, filled with emotion, said, "I can tell if he was still alive, he'd be my best friend." The tears continued to flow as my husband hugged Matthew and we both told him he was right. We knew Tommy would love to be his friend.

I told them I believe Tommy is an angel and here with us this day, filled with pride and gratitude that they spent months collecting these items and monies from their entire school just for the animals. They had chosen this shelter as their Penny/Harvesting Project. They made three paintings. One was for this shelter, another for Tommy's school P.S. 36, and one for their school. Every student in the school participated in the project by submitting drawings of animals. This committee chose the ones to be used in each painting, and then every child in the school assisted in the painting. Each picture had Tommy and Sophie in the center with Tommy's coffee can. Some paintings had different animals, but they all had the Rainbow Bridge over the heads of Tommy and the animals. They knew Tommy was at the other side of the Rainbow Bridge greeting the deceased animals that crossed over to animal heaven. Is this not the most beautiful story you ever heard?

After a very meaningful, emotional experience, the students gave me a huge group hug that lasted a long time. We threw kisses to each other as they drove away. God is so good! God bless those special teachers and principal, especially the project's coordinator, Rose Marie Hughes. We will never forget that day! I pray that God watches over all those children, their families, and their animals, especially the Chinese boy's dog that he had to leave in China. We are all connected with the one word that best describes Tommy—*love*!

The national American Society for the Prevention of Cruelty to Animals (ASPCA) gave a hefty donation to the animal shelter in Tommy's name after reading about Tommy's dedication to animals. They are planning their annual fund-raiser in Manhattan and asked Maria and Tom's permission to name an award after Tommy because of the way he lived his life. It is the ASPCA Tommy Monahan Kid of the Year Award. They believe Tommy epitomizes what the award is all about. The recipient will be someone who aids in the protection of an animal in duress. The award will be presented at the Annual National ASPCA luncheon held in the Rainbow Room at Rockefeller Center.

Mike Daley, journalist for the New York *Daily News,* has been a friend of our son Craig since the Watt Street fire, March 28, 1996, when Craig's firehouse Ladder 5/Engine 24 lost our close friend Captain John Drennan and firefighters Chris Seidenberg and Jimmy Young. Mike covered Craig's involvement on 9/11 with his pickup truck "The War Wagon," as well as Ladder 5/Engine 24's devastating losses at the Deutsche Building fire shortly after Tommy's death. As all our good friends did, Mike came to Tommy's wake. He then published a moving article about Tommy's book *My Dog Sophie.* Mike brought Tommy's story to everyone's attention since the *News* is published up and down the East Coast and available worldwide on the Internet. His personal focus on Tommy's book was quite emotional and brought Tommy's love of his dog to all. Mike described Tommy's book in its entirety, and he commented that "Uncle Craig (after sharing the book with a mourner) placed the book back in the coffin with Tommy along with the ashes of his terrier Sophie and his coffee can of donations for the animal shelter."

Fishing with Grandpa, Dad, Uncle Craig, and cousins

CHAPTER *10:*
Additional Memorials

"Rejoice Always."
(1 Thessalonians 5:16)

At the beginning of 2008, the South Shore Lion's Club had a town hall meeting and invited Tommy's family as guests of honor. Prior to the meeting, our family met privately with New York City Mayor Michael Bloomberg. His Honor interviewed Tom, Maria, Kevin, Ashley, and Gabrielle. The mayor asked Grandpa if he'd always lived on Staten Island. Grandpa replied, "I was born and raised here; I just haven't grown up yet." The mayor appreciated Grandpa's humor and was very empathetic and gracious to our family. Our family sat at a front table with the councilmen. All New York City department commissioners attended the meeting.

The National Humanitarians Circle of Courage of 2007 Award was presented to our family in honor of Tommy's bravery and dedication to come to the aid of all animals in distress.

On February 16, neighbors of Tom and Maria hosted a benefit to help the family rebuild their home, hoping to replace all that was lost in the fire. Saint Joseph-Saint Thomas' pastor, Monsignor E. Whalen, enthusiastically allowed them the use of the gymnasium, with the wholehearted support of the girls' basketball team, which had been scheduled to use the gym that evening. The entire sports program, family school association, and many individual parishioners came out in droves to do all they could to make the benefit a huge success. Grandpa Monahan, born and raised in this parish, had never seen an event there to compare with the enormity of this one. Volunteers gathered and set up seventy-five baskets to be raffled off. There was a very large list of Island-wide donors who without hesitation gave generously to this event. What started out to be a dinner-dance (which normally draws between two hundred and two hundred forty people) turned out to be a seated dinner for over five hundred people.

The outside walls and school hallway were packed with people filled with the spirit of goodwill. The love that flowed like a silent river energized every single soul that was present. It was an event beyond anyone's expectations. The best part was, despite the overcrowded gym, everyone was grateful to be there. Senator Andrew Lanza and Councilman Lou Tobacco joined the festivities and humbly mixed among the crowd. Sal Cassano, chief of the Fire Department City of New York (FDNY), along with our faithful firefighters from Ladder 5/ Engine 24 and their families, were present. Al Petrocelli (retired FDNY chief) was there to set up. The benefit committee (none of whom are parishioners of our parish)—George Hopkins, Jim Monreale, Tom Bradley, and Bob Ryan—were overwhelmed with gratitude for all who helped and participated in any fashion.

The dedication and love for our family shown by those men and their families, as well as all of their Saint Joseph-Saint Thomas workers, are what true Christianity is all about. God is so good to us by allowing us to be members of this very generous community. We were amazed at the energy, dedication, and love displayed by Sister Michael, a Presentation nun dedicated to service in our parish. She was one of the first volunteers on the scene and one of the last to leave, barely able to stand or talk. She was our evening's photographer, capturing the enormity of the event. God bless every single volunteer and their families for doing all that was necessary to make this event as spectacular as it was.

I was asked to speak on behalf of our family after our daughter Terry accepted Tommy's award from the National Humane Society. Maria asked Terry to accept the award since Terry was Tommy's second mom. Terry's son Joey was very close to Tommy. They were closer than brothers and shared the same interests; Tommy idolized his twelve-year-old cousin. They did everything together, and Terry treated Tommy like a son. Her tearful acceptance speech touched all present as she shared Joey's reaction to Tommy's death. As per Maria's request, I read the eulogy of Earth Camp counselor Ryan Hepworth. The eulogy can be read in its entirety in the preface of this book. It clearly epitomizes the essence of Tommy.

The sports program director of our CYO teams, Frank Di Candido, along with his sports committee dedicated their yearly Sports Program Mass in memory of four individuals they lost during the year. They remembered Tommy, ten-year old Joey Verdino, Anthony Nuccio (Tommy's teammate's dad), and Marilyn Blohm (the mom of an eighth grader in our school). It was a beautiful Mass, and I thought quite interesting that the sports program lost a family (one dad, one mom, and two sons). Our parish is a close family, and everyone has been there for each of these families in their grief. I believe those two deceased parents are there for Tommy and Joey as those boys play ball in heaven. I can visualize Joey teaching Tommy great moves on the baseball field, and Tommy showing Joey how to be a great goalie. I also find it interesting that in 2007 our church, St. *Joseph* and St. *Thomas,* lost two boys: *Joseph* and *Thomas.*

Opening day for the Saint Joseph-Saint Thomas CYO Soccer Tournament was held at Monsignor Farrell High School in memory of Tommy. Following the opening prayer by Father John Palatucci, there was a moment of silence in honor of Tommy. Tommy's team played the first seventy-two seconds one man short and retired his number, 72. Tommy and Maria donated the proceeds to the CYO league.

The Staten Island United Travel Soccer Club hosted the first annual Tommy Monahan Memorial Tournament on June 21 and 22, presented by Manfredi's Auto Group. There were sixty-six sponsors, and it was held at the College of Staten Island. The referees graciously donated their time from nine o'clock a.m. to four o'clock p.m. both days. The professional New York Red Bulls were in attendance, donating their time; autographing shirts, soccer balls, and sneakers; as well as donating ten tickets to two of their games. There were raffles of all kinds. Teams came from other boroughs as well as New Jersey to play. Our grandson Joey Quercia, Tommy's best-buddy cousin, played on the Battle of Monmouth Raptors Travel Team from New Jersey. Their team was an invited guest to the tournament and played Staten Island United Red Bulls and Regional Development School. It was quite an emotional day for all. Through the tears of grief, there were moments of pride and happiness watching Tommy's and Joey's teams give the best games they could give.

The deep pain of loss never goes away, but we are comforted by the presence of all our grandchildren, most of whom were able to attend this tournament. The emotions began as we approached the entrance to the college, where there was a sign to greet all the teams with directions to the field of the Tommy Monahan Soccer Tournament. On the fence of the field itself stood two professional signs, one with a life-size picture of Tommy at a travel soccer game in Virginia in which he participated. The other sign listed the names of all sixty-six sponsors. It was a most memorable event. Proceeds went to the Staten Island United Travel Team League in memory of Tommy.

The Staten Island Museum established a five-year scholarship program in Tommy's memory so other youth who exhibit his enthusiasm for knowledge may also experience some of the excitement that Tommy found at Earth Camp. Earth Camp was the perfect environment for Tommy to shine in the crowd. He knew so much about Mother Earth and her creatures, loving them all no matter how small or large. We are so grateful he had those experiences and believe he's with Steve Irwin and all the rest among every creature he was ever curious about. We believe his spirit comes to us in the forms of some of those creatures.

On June 6, 2008, the Staten Island Recreational Association Inc. (SIRA) held their first annual fund-raiser to benefit the HOOPH (Helping Others Overcome Personal Handicaps) program. The staff utilizes horseback riding to accomplish their goal of bonding their clients with the horses. It is a very therapeutic experience. The HOOPH program works with accredited therapists to help their participants improve speech, muscle coordination, balance, sensory awareness, and self-esteem, as well as provide a one-of-a-kind recreational opportunity to a population that has such limits. On behalf of SIRA, our neighbor Barbara LoNigro requested the family's permission to honor Tommy's memory by naming their first annual volunteer of the year award in his name. I was honored to participate in the presentation of the Thomas Monahan V Perpetual Memorial Trophy to Alexis Brown and Kayla Wood, the two young, outstanding volunteers of the year. It was a memorable evening, and I felt Tommy smiling down with pride. As an equestrian rider for the past two years, our eight-year-old Gabrielle is looking forward to being old enough to volunteer for HOOPH.

There is a star named for Tommy, and his family has a framed map guiding them to his star.

A tree has been planted in Tommy's name in a devastated forest outside of Yellowstone National Park.

Cousin Craig, friends Gavin Monreale and
Brendon Walsh, Tommy, and Cousin Joey

Tommy, Sophie, Gabrielle

"C'mon, Mom, can I keep him?"

Chapter 11:
Through the Eyes of the Children

"Dear Friends, let us love one another, because love comes from God. Whoever loves is a child of God and knows God."
(1 John 4:7)

The children's messages were, of course, the most meaningful. Carolyn Oglio is the leader of our parish's children's bereavement program, the Little Angels Group. She is also the director of the Rainbows program for the Archdiocese of New York. Rainbows in an international bereavement program for children. Carolyn worked with the children in our religious education program to help them get answers, share feelings, and have a format to face and deal with their feelings about Tommy's death. She also worked with the teachers and school psychologist of P.S. 36, Lucy Zammit Waters, giving those students the same experience to work through their grief.

All of those children made us such heartfelt cards and messages. They soothed our souls, eased our broken hearts, and often made us smile or laugh. Carolyn presented us with a very full loose-leaf notebook of messages from the children of both schools. Here is a glimpse of some of those messages. Interestingly, the same themes were revealed over and over again. It is quite obvious these children knew Tommy well. In fact, at times, better than we did.

I Remember ...
He always had a smile on his face... He was nice and always laughed... He had freckles on his face... I miss him a lot, and I

46

know you do, too… He would volunteer to read in religion and be respectful to one another. I think he had blue eyes… He had freckles on his cheeks but not his nose… He was excited about CCD. He loved his teacher, Mrs. Nickolauk… very intelligent, very smart, handsome, attractive boy … He was an awesome boy… a great kid … He would make the teacher go mad, and we would all laugh about it, but he was a good boy, not a bad boy… He was a good friend… the time we played soccer together—I knew you were the best player on the team… Me and Tommy were in a soccer game. We were right at the goal. Were passing and passing. I passed it to him, and he scored… I was so happy for him… playing sports like kickball, baseball, and football. We also played army, and we tried to find animals because he loved and cared about them and never let anyone hurt them… Tom was a very good soccer player, and he would help me in the games because I was goalie. I'm sad, really sad, and I miss him very much. Go, X-Men. Tom was my best friend. Go, X-Men!… when Thomas always let people borrow his stuff. One time Thomas let me borrow his pencil at the end of CCD. He said Everrett, you can keep that. I said thank you Thomas… When you drove me to all the soccer practices and when you told me what your lizard was like and thank you for teaching me some moves. You let me play with you a lot, and I will always remember because we are best friends… I know it's hard not to think of him. I felt that way too. My uncle died too, and it was hard to let that go. So you don't have to worry, he is still with you in heaven looking after you… It was when we went strawberry picking. My mom had come along on the trip to help. Thomas had asked my mom if she could help him pick some nice strawberries to bring home for his sister… The time when we were playing kickball Thomas caught a catch that no one ever caught. Was the class clown too. He was so funny you couldn't believe it. I wish you were still at school… I used to share gum with him on the school bus. I used to save a piece for him when he gets on the bus… when Tom won the lizard in class, and he was so happy that he said that he will take good care of the lizard. When he said when we play kickball I will make your team win. So he did that day. I can't believe that someone that age could go thru something like that. My best friend Thomas. I miss you… a lot of good times about Thomas like when he wanted to be funny. So he decided to make a mustache on his face. He got a sharpy and started! It was so funny. That day we had a substitute teacher. She probably said or did something to make Thomas look. The teacher looked at him and she told him to wipe it off. Thomas had to wipe it off near the closet window. While he was doing that, the class was cracking up. That day the class and I had a very good laugh… The class is not the same… When Thomas said a flying bear would come in from the window. Everyone laughed. He sat right next to me. He is in heaven now with God… when we were walking back to the classroom from lunch and Thomas was humming a tune. Then he started singing it out loud to himself but lowly. I asked him what he was singing and he replied, "Rainbow Monkeys." I cracked up… when we were sitting on the rug and we were playing a multiplication game and we had boards in front of us. Thomas picked up his board and wrote "Go girl power."… when Thomas quizzed me. He asked me what kind of tree smells like peanut butter and jelly. I didn't know so I gave up. He said it was the Atlantis Tree. He was very smart. My heart ached. My family was so depressed… when one day when we were on our way back to class from recess. Thomas picked up a few acorns and when we were on the rug he put the acorns in his ears. Later Mrs. Jelicks said, "Thomas, get that out of your ear." Thomas said, "What, I'm nuts." The whole class starting laughing. He was a funny kid… when he put sticky notes on his ears to show everyone he has earrings. It was very funny. I miss Thomas… I will always remember Tommy catching green frogs at Long Pond and playing Frisbee together. We once teamed at Lemon Creek and caught the most fish that day. A good friend, Tommy will be greatly missed by everyone at Earth Camp… When me and Thomas used to sit on the bus together. We use to talk about Pokemon and we use to duel. In Kindergarten we use to sit and talk and play but this is to you guys. You just got to remember that even though you can't see him, he is always going to be with you and in your hearts—so don't be down. He's watching over you just like God.

Tommy's cousin Russell was on the yearbook committee for Good Shepherd's School in Nutley, New Jersey. The committee had a page in this year's school yearbook dedicated to the memory of Tommy. The dedication page told Tommy's story. It was quite touching and was appreciated by our family.

On the day Tommy died, his best friend Gavin wrote him a letter and placed it in Tommy's casket at the wake.

Dear Tommy, I miss you so much. I was crying a lot. I hope you are having a very good time. How is your great Grandfather and how are you? Love, your best friend, Gavin

The following letter was written by Gavin on September 28, 2008, before he came to visit me and share his feelings about Tommy, knowing I was writing this book. We had a special visit.

Dear Tommy, I miss you so much and I miss you when we used to play kickball with each other. I also miss when we used to play video games with each other and soccer. I loved how we dressed up as nerds on Halloween. We had the best costumes even your mom said it. From your friend, Gavin.

Gavin's sister Lauren Monreale wrote Tommy a letter that is in his *Memories Book*:

Dear Tommy—It has been a tough time for us down on Earth. Your family, your friends, your neighbors, and people you have never met. We all will miss you for the rest of our lives on Earth, but I know that someday we will all see you again. I know right now, that you are in God's arms looking upon us with angels, saints and God. You would be proud because everyone is donating all that they can to your family and to the Staten Island Animal Care Center. You are famous down here. We all love you and miss you. You were like family, a brother to me. I'm glad we share the memories that we have. See you again one day Tom. Enjoy life in Heaven, and say, "hello" to God for me. I love you and miss you. We can still hear your laughter and see your face. Talk to you soon. We love you and miss you. Love, your neighbor, Lauren.

Missing You
By Lauren Monreale and Nicole Turturro
I Think about you day and night.
Life without you is a fright.
I remember the day when you stepped away.
I want to hear you say,
"It's okay."
I really wish you could stay.
Although it's hard for me to face it,
I know I must accept it.
I love everything about you
and your caring heart too.
God broke my heart to prove to me,
He only takes the best.
(An Ode to Thomas Paul Monahan and Thomas J. Turturro)

One of Tommy's neighbors named Ashlee wrote this poem:

Tommy

Thank you for being my friend.

Thank you for always being nice to me and making me laugh.

Thank you for always choosing my side in kickball.

Thank you for laughing at Ava when everyone else got mad.

Thank you for being the first person to show me the right way to kick a soccer ball.

Thank you for teaching me about bugs, insects, snakes, and animals that I would never touch without you by my side.

Thank you for swimming with me until our hands were prunes.

Thank you for all the memories.

I will always love you… Ashlee

These children are truly the great leaders of tomorrow. We treasure their words.

When I told Gabrielle I was writing a book, she told me how Tommy liked to go to the Seguine Stables with her. Gabrielle takes equestrian riding lessons, and Tommy would go to collect the fallen peacock feathers at the stable. Gabrielle asked that I print a poem that she wrote for Tommy:

Oh Soccer Shirt
Oh soccer shirt, Oh soccer shirt,
I miss you, I miss you.
You were my family's good luck charm.
When I saw you in the coffin you were there Tommy.
I LOVE YOU AND I MISS YOU TOMMY ......Gab

Gabrielle has decided to play soccer and is doing so well. She joined a different team than her brother's, and she loves it. She requested number 6, one of her brother's numbers, but it was unavailable. The number she was given is 51. Her dad pointed out that 5 + 1 = 6, which pleases her.

The number of children who attended Tommy's wake was enormous. It's just not normal! It should not be! No child should have to attend the wake of another. Life can be so unfair, yet it is what it is and we have to face that reality and deal with it—like it or not!

It breaks my heart every time I think of Gabrielle and her cousins having to deal with the reality—Tommy has died! Tommy's friends and classmates should not have to be living with this reality also. Yet, thanks to Carolyn Oglio, the teachers at P.S. 36, along with the school psychologist Lucy Zammit Waters and St. Joseph-St. Thomas religious education principal Elizabeth Brim and their devoted staff, the children were given support and guidance in addition to what they received from their parents. Hopefully, these unfortunate circumstances helped those precious souls process their painful feelings. I know their presence and support helped us get through our pain.

We kept all the letters, cards, messages, and drawings that were written by a few hundred children that lifted up our broken spirits. Tommy and Gabrielle's friends' messages were particularly meaningful and precious. The school and CCD classmates and children from schools we did not know were amazingly creative and emotionally supportive. God bless the children, each and every one of them.

Gavin and Lauren's mom, Patty Monreale, shared her thoughts:

BEST FRIENDS

There's something about having your best friend live right next door that makes life just a little more special.

That's how it was with my son Gavin and Tommy. They were best friends since the time they could walk and talk. They would often knock on each other's back doors early in the morning with their pajamas on and hang out for hours without changing into their regular clothes.

They never missed each other's birthday parties. They looked forward to planning their Halloween costumes every year. They always brought each other something back from vacation. Tommy was always the first person that Gavin wanted to show a new toy or share his good news with and Tommy was always very receptive. There were times where Gavin would try to jump out of the car before it stopped to run to Tommy's house with his new treasure or his good news about winning a soccer or football game.

Tommy and Gavin shared a very special bond. Their conversations consisted of talk about soccer, baseball cards, football, bugs, cartoons, and video games. They spent endless days riding bikes, swimming in the pool, watching cartoons, trading cards, playing video games, digging in the dirt, catching bugs, and playing manhunt and kickball in the street.

Life will never be the same without Tommy next door, but Gavin will forever be grateful to his best friend for making life just a little more special for nine years.

Thank you and God bless you, Tommy.

Another neighbor, the mother of Tommy's good friend Jonathan, wrote a message in the classmates' memory book. It is *so Tommy.*

I remember ... *Tommy getting so excited because those ugly crunchy beetles had made their home in my tree. He must have gathered at least two dozen beetles or shells. On my tree they were starting to get out of his reach so I had to give him a ladder. A bomb could have gone off and Tommy would never have heard it because he was so involved with the beetles. God Bless! Heaven has a beautiful Angel.* ***We love you and miss you!*** *—Erin Ready*

The *Staten Island Advance* printed a twelve-page guest book online where concerned readers sent our family messages to console us.

We were so grateful to each and every person. We received letters and cards from over eighteen hundred people. Our hearts were truly touched by each gesture of compassion, especially those from the children. We kept every card and letter. Generally speaking, most of us question what is happening to this world, especially due to all the wars, terrorism, and acts of violence wherever you look. Yet it is our experience, as a result of Tommy's death, that people are loving, compassionate, and generous beyond belief. We will never forget their goodness. We heard from strangers across this nation.

FOR   Tommy

LOVE

JOHN CONNOLLY
6 years old

We miss you.

Kathleen Connolly 8yrs old

CHAPTER *12:*
Parental Reflections

"I have the strength to face all conditions
by the power that Christ gives me."
(Phililippians 4:13)

It's August 18, a sunny summer day, and as I sit on our front porch praying the rosary, I thank God for this beautiful day. As I ask the Blessed Mother to watch over my family, I am particularly concerned about the health of my son Tom and my husband. They have both been experiencing the physical symptoms so prevalent with stress. My husband has been under the doctor's care for months now trying to determine the origin of his physical symptoms. An infection seems to be playing havoc with his body as he undergoes treatment for his skin cancer and sinus infection. Our son has an appointment with the doctor this afternoon. I'm grateful he's doing the best he can to take care of himself, particularly for Gabrielle's and Maria's sakes. While talking to him the other day about my decision to write this book, we talked about the night Tommy died and reflected on circumstances prior to his death.

My son shared, "Never in a million years would I ever go to the beach with Tommy at night. However, one night Tommy kept asking me to go." In hindsight, only now does he understand why he allowed Tommy to win him over. "We walked along the beach in the dark to collect driftwood for his anoles to climb on in their cage. We grabbed all sizes, so they'd have many choices for climbing. I'm so glad I gave in to him that night."

Last fall, en route to a soccer game, for another unknown reason our son spontaneously told Tommy to "Play like it is your last game." Our son found himself saying that each time Tommy went to play soccer. It turned out while at his last game with his travel team at Midland Beach, Tommy *scored* two goals and *assisted* in the other two goals his team scored. They won that game, and Tommy was in all his glory. He wore his medal to school the next day. That was *his* day! He played his best, and his team was so proud of him. That happened on December 8, the feast of the Immaculate Conception. It does not surprise me that Tommy had superhuman power on that day—his very last game. Another favorite day of his was when he was asked by an older tournament team to play as their guest in Virginia Beach. He played sensationally that day also. Tommy's love for soccer came from his mom, who actively encouraged his dedication to the game.

My son shared how difficult it was to go back to their house on Princewood Avenue the night Tommy died. Our daughter Terry drove his family to our house after leaving the hospital and took Tom to his house to make sure it was locked up after the firemen left. He hoped to get some phone numbers and to leave a message on his job's answering machine informing them he wouldn't be at work that day. He was concerned that his boss's son Patrick might need their work van. In Tom's intense grief, he didn't want to leave the message of his son's death on the answering machine. His boss, Warren Johnson, and Warren's family have been his good friends since childhood. Obviously, our son was in deep shock and the deepest pain a parent can have, yet he thought about the Johnson family at the same time. Tom remembered the difficulty days later when he had to call the office to say he had one less dependent to be reflected in his paycheck.

Terry reported how difficult it was after dropping Gabrielle, Ashley, and Maria at our house after leaving the hospital. As they drove onto Princewood Avenue, the media were surrounding the house, along with the fire marshall's trucks. The house was lit up like broad daylight from the television vans that were taping the house fire.

When they approached the house, Tom had to show his identification before they let him in. They let Tom go into the basement to retrieve the insurance papers. There was two feet of water that he waded through in his pajamas. Knowing that the family was still in their pajamas and had no access to their clothes, Terry looked for clothes that might have been left in the washer or dryer. Unfortunately, there were none because Tom had put them away the previous day, before the fire. Arriving at our house, Tom changed into his dad's dry clothes.

I will never forget the day I walked into the kitchen a few days after the funeral. Our son Tom was sitting at the kitchen table staring at a form he had just received in the mail. Tears were pouring out of his eyes so heavily he could hardly see the words. It was a bill from the fire department requesting details about his son's death. How insensitive. It was obvious the form had been mailed out the day after Tommy's death. There was a second bill for the ambulance that Maria and Gabrielle were in.

Tom's heart was ripped open again, forced to relive those horrifying moments so close to Tommy's death. He lost his son, his house, and most of their belongings. Not knowing where to go from here and forced to pay these large bills, he was despondent.

He struggled through the form even though his father offered to help him. He said he had to do this himself. Our hearts were bleeding for him. This just was not normal. This should not be happening, but it was. He paid Tommy's bill with anger and much hurt, but did not see the sense of paying Maria and Gabrielle's bill.

The circumstances around Maria and Gabrielle's use of the ambulance did not warrant payment. Right after Tommy's ambulance left Princewood Avenue, Maria went to be with Gabrielle at a neighbor's house. When Maria learned that Tommy had been revived and was going to the burn center, she expressed a desire to go to the hospital to be with Tommy. She stated the FDNY ambulance staff said they were going to drive to the burn center and she was welcome to ride with them. She accepted their offer, not aware she would be charged for "the ride."

Maria and Tom sent that bill back, stating they did not think they should pay that large bill. Their hurt was justified anger. Maria said, "How dare they? I could have asked a neighbor to drive me there." When informed of the circumstances, the FDNY quickly remedied the situation.

When grieving the death of a child, we don't have the luxury of thinking about these situations intellectually. We are not robots. In the midst of terrifying grief like ours, the bereaved have to deal with understandable bills from various institutions. As a mom and a grandma, I hope that someday the systems mandated to send such necessary paperwork to the bereaved can find a more sensitive approach.

Mom, Dad, Tommy, brother Kevin, sisters Gabrielle and Ashley

Kindergarten graduation with Mom

Returning dead shark found on beach to complete circle of life

CHAPTER *13:*
A Grandmother's Grief

*"So always trust the Lord because he
is forever our mighty rock."*
(Isaiah 26:4)

The stages of grief include denial, disorganization, anger, guilt and bargaining, physical and emotional distress, depression, loss and loneliness, withdrawal, acceptance, and reaching out. Our family experienced *complicated grief*; grief that is coupled with depression. *Abnormal grief* is grief accompanied with multiple losses. That certainly applies to us. Our family lost a child, a house, a dog, furniture, clothes, pictures, multiple personal mementoes, toys, and the feeling of security.

My husband and I experienced *disenfranchised grief*; grief that does not receive societal acknowledgement. A grandparent's grief is rarely considered and the usual supports may not be available. The resources for grandparents are very limited. I was frustrated and felt very isolated in my search for literature to help myself. My husband and I were grateful when family and friends acknowledged our special pain. Losing our beloved Tommy was bad enough, but watching our children's pain was unbearable.

Thank God Tom and Maria stayed with us the first four months. We're grateful to them for choosing to be with us at this time. After they left, I started looking at my own grief. I had been too busy to put much thought into my own feelings. My journal helped to begin that process. I realized how important prayer and my faith were to my survival. Of course, as is typical, I also got in touch with my depression, but not until around June.

As a bereavement minister for years, I have reached out to others suffering depression as a result of the death of their loved ones. I found myself experiencing the same symptoms I taught others about. Despite my prayers and strong faith, I was experiencing intense grief emotions. I had a hole in my stomach, a physical pain in my heart, and at times uncontrollable tears (especially in church, where I feel safe and closest to God). At times I experienced shallow breathing and frequently had to take slow, deep breaths to calm down. I was overwhelmed with fear about what was going to happen to my family. It was frightening, and I was so powerless. I was crushed with the loss of Tommy. I do believe he is in heaven and happier than he would be on this earth, but I struggled with the helplessness that I couldn't change reality.

Many people have questioned why I'm not disillusioned with my faith and angry at God for not saving our grandson. I was doing everything I could to stay focused and hold on to my faith. I believe it was Tommy's time to die; and although I'm often hysterical over the way it happened, I still do believe he's happy in heaven. How could I consider *losing my faith?* I need it more now than ever before.

Along with other prayers, I frequently say the Serenity Prayer. Knowing I had to take care of myself in order to take care of my family, I returned to the YMCA for my swimming exercises. As difficult as it was, due to no motivation, I had to go back to my routine daily swim and aquatics.

I returned to the YMCA one week after the funeral. I reluctantly awoke early to get back to my schedule. As I entered the building at six o'clock in the morning to register at the front desk, the receptionist came from behind the desk to express condolences. I never knew her name up until that moment; we only greeted each other casually each morning. She had read about the fire and tragic death of Tommy. With tears in her eyes, Karen placed a silver Serenity Prayer bracelet on my arm that she had taken off her own arm. She tearfully explained that I would receive peace while wearing it.

I couldn't believe this stranger was so compassionate and sensitive to my needs. The comfort and peace that this bracelet has brought me each and every day is amazing. Karen is one of the angels God sent my way down here on earth. I wore the bracelet every day until it broke. I took it to my jeweler, who was kind enough to repair it on the spot. I could not leave it anywhere. Frank Anson and his employees were extremely sensitive to my needs, reinforcing my bracelet with determination to ease my pain. They were also one of the most generous donors to the benefit the neighbors held for our family. The security I received from them and my bracelet was so helpful. Whenever stressed, I hold the Serenity Prayer charm in my hand and say the prayer; immediately peace flows through my body. My friend Janet Cote, my niece Donna's mom, gave me two religious bracelets that also bring me comfort each day. I received a beautiful rosary bracelet from my close friend Mary Ann Walsh. God is good!

My friend Jessica Drennan Westra lives in the Berkshires. She sent me healing gifts to soothe my hurting soul. Her first gift was a blue, hand-knit "cocoon scarf" made of cashmere and silk to keep me warm during those cold days of grief. I understand those yarns are very difficult to work with. She even offered to clean and repair it when needed. Jessica is not Catholic but heard my plea for everyone to pray the rosary for Tommy. Hearing how important the rosary was to me and wanting to help in any way to ease our pain, Jessica bought a rosary and learned how to pray it. Those of us who pray the rosary know how comforted Jessica becomes when she prays it. I was so grateful for her recent visit with her children, Vivian and Gerrit, and her mom, Vina, our close friend for years.

The most effective relief from my depression is our grandchildren. I've had little energy, but I love seeing our precious little angels. Gabrielle asked me to have a girls' sleepover. I didn't think I'd have the energy but felt it was important to do, not just for Gabrielle, but for the other girls as well.

In the past, I would periodically have a girls' sleepover and, at other times, a boys' sleepover. The younger grandchildren love to be together at Grandma and Grandpa's. On July 17, the girls came over to our house.

It turned out that Melissa needed me to babysit the morning of July 18, so we invited six-year-old Johnny to the sleepover along with his sisters, Kayla and Kathleen, and, of course, Gabrielle. Unfortunately for us, cousin Catie was out of town with her mom those two days. We invited Craig (five years old) and Christian (three years old) to join us during the day. Watching them interact so well, listening to their hearty laughter, and watching them splashing away in our pool was so healing. I was so glad fourteen-year-old Christina came along. The younger girls look up to Christina, and she was my helper in the pool when I took the younger ones up to the house to the bathroom. Eight-year-old Kathleen was constantly asking to help me when I was cooking, serving, and setting up the beds.

The next morning Joey came over, and we all took a walk to Tommy's Pond together: Christina, Kayla, Gabrielle, Kathleen, Johnny, Craig, Christian, Joey, and I. Joey helped the younger boys as they walked on the top of the wall. We all walked the paths looking for the turtles' eggs that were there days earlier and listened to God's creatures serenading us. We stopped to talk to Tommy and said the Hail Mary together, thanking the Blessed Mother for taking care of Tommy for us. It was a special moment.

While preparing for bed, long after the boys had gone home, someone spotted a spider on the ceiling. The children believed the spider was Tommy—crashing the girls' sleepover. I used a broom to gently remove the spider, telling him he knows better than to crash the girls' party, and placed the spider outside. A large beetle was spotted on the ceiling a little while later. "Maybe Tommy came back as a bigger bug," someone said. It's so comforting to watch the children's hope. Everlasting life is real: they believe they will see him again, and they see his spirit in many ways. He didn't die forever—he just died as we knew him, and he is always with us.

Thank God our faith is so strong. I can't imagine getting through this grief without the Lord. We also thank God for the support of our family and friends, especially my sister-in-law, Grace, and friend for over fifty years Betty Stroh. They were there for us every day whenever we needed them. Actually, we were offered help from many people every day.

My friend and our church organist, Dolores Talley, along with the Bereavement Support Group we cofacilitate, have been a tremendous support to me. Dolores was smart and kind enough to suggest I take a break from running the group at that time. Her concern was that I needed to put all my energies into my own recovery. Committed to the group, I decided to give it a try. I knew the group members were suffering my loss along with me. That's what good groups do! We are there for ourselves, but at the same time sensitive to each other's needs. The healing is in the sharing.

As painful as it was, I attended the group. It's amazing how well the group works. The group members, with guidance from Dolores and Carolyn Oglio, were there for me. When I expressed concern that they were not getting what they needed themselves, they unanimously responded, "It gives us pleasure to give back to you what you have given to us."

Ronnie, a mom whose son died under tragic circumstances, invited the entire group to her house for dinner. She claimed she was not a cook or entertainer, but her gratitude to the group for how they helped her motivated her to entertain us.

It was a beautiful evening. We had such fun while eating her delicious home cooking and laughing and sharing. At times, the tears flowed. I was not in the mood to go to dinner when initially invited, but was so grateful for Ronnie's gesture that I went. I only went to support Ronnie's efforts, yet I received such blessings from her and each group member. Our dinner went on for hours. God is so good. I am so grateful for this powerful group.

It's amazing how angry grief can make us. It would come in waves, but fortunately I've had enough training to recognize when it crept up on me. Much of the time, I would find myself projecting my anger at my husband. I'd criticize everything he did or said and then find myself justifying my behavior. I felt like I was drowning myself in a cesspool of negativity. Feeling completely hopeless, I wanted to run away from myself.

Thank God I continued seeking help and reached out to my good friend and mentor Mary Ann Walsh. We would meet at the YMCA early in the morning, and while swimming together, I'd do more crying and sharing. Her unconditional love and guidance put things into perspective. I'd leave there feeling energized and centered. I'd meet my husband at church where we attend daily Mass, and then we'd go home for breakfast together.

While processing my emotions, I realized I had stopped journaling. I was allowing the negativity around me to become internalized. I struggled to release the negativity. While swimming my half mile each morning, I worked to physically release my anger. With these efforts and the power of prayer, my depression began to lift. Our only salvation is letting our negativity go. It's toxic and unproductive and only hurts ourselves.

I had to practice what I taught my clients for years as a trained counselor as well as what I taught the bereaved, whom I have worked with these past ten years. It's a humbling experience practicing what you preach. At the same time, it is encouraging. I'm better now at recognizing and validating my emotions, whatever they are, and choosing healthier ways to deal with them. However, I recognize that awareness doesn't happen just because I want it to. It happened because I worked hard at each step of the way. Honesty, sharing, listening, and letting go are essential in working through grief.

Earth Camp catch

CHAPTER 14:
A Fitting Tribute

"In the sight of the Angels I will sing your praises Lord."
(Psalms 138:1)

Three weeks after Tommy's tenth birthday, I found myself avoiding writing about that day even though Tommy would have believed it was his best birthday ever due to the events of that special day. It was extremely emotional but a great celebration. Still, we would have moved the world if we could bring him back and just have a simple pool party with hot dogs and homemade brownies.

The weather forecast wasn't hopeful, with the expectation of rain in the afternoon. Before dawn, at approximately five o'clock on the morning of Tommy's birthday, Tom and Maria were sitting on the front steps of their new home, which sits approximately three hundred feet from the ocean beachfront. They were reflecting on his day. Each had a cup of coffee in hand. Somewhere over the beach, an enormously loud display of fireworks went off. They had no idea where they came from. A beautiful beginning to the day celebrating Tommy's birth.

At daybreak, two tankers passed through the channel directly in front of their house. Periodically tankers go through this channel, but they had never seen two ships cross next to each other in this narrow channel nor arrive that early in the morning either. There was no question in Mom's and Dad's minds that their little boy was with them and demonstrating his power.

The Oglio family had the 8:00 a.m. Mass said for Tommy's birthday. It was a beautifully inspirational Mass concelebrated by Monsignor

Whalen, Father Roesch, and our new Deacon Villanueva. Monsignor Whalen personalized the homily. We were so grateful. I had breakfast following the Mass. Later that morning, I took a walk to Tommy's Pond to pray the rosary.

At five o'clock that evening, Monsignor Whalen blessed the new tombstone with a beautiful prayer service. We were grateful it didn't rain, although some drizzling appeared briefly. I believe the angels were crying for us. Many gifts adorned the stone. What caught my eye was the small, seashelled box with a letter to Tommy written by a neighborhood friend, Samantha DeFilippo:

"I never thought I would see this day when you wouldn't be here to show me the way. You taught me all different things about nature, between what was right and what was wrong. You always had a way, but that was before you were gone.

You always made me smile. I don't know how you did it, but not sure if I really care. But I know that you are with me. I know that you are there. I cry and cry for what seems forever, but I know some day will come and we will be together. One day you were there, the next you had to leave. I don't know what to do, I don't know what to believe.

But I kept wondering why. Why this and why that, why you had to go. I tried my hardest not to let my feelings show. It took me quite a while to accept that you had died. With all that, I want to say I miss you and good-bye."

After our good-byes at the cemetery, we all went to Walker Pond, where the Parks Department had built a beautiful dock in Tommy's name. Our whole family was present this day, as well as Maria's family, Tommy's friends from Princewood Avenue and their families, and some of our neighbors. Walker Pond is truly a hidden treasure on Staten Island. Without direction, you would not see the path leading to the pond from the parking lot. As you walk into the clearing at the far left-hand corner of the parking lot, the woods begin to open. When you walk the path, you can see the pond through the trees. What a perfect spot for Tommy's dock. Knowing Tommy, you could feel his excitement and wonder watching this day. This place is all about him. The path opens up where this large sturdy dock floats upon the water's edge.

Straight across the pond there was a beautiful, tall blue heron, standing still as a statue in the water. Some thought it was a statue. Our family knew it was real and another sign that Tommy was there. The pond was covered with lily pads. I only saw one white flower among all the lily pads. That flower was approximately five feet directly in front of the sign on the dock:

"Take only memories, leave nothing but footprints."
—Chief Seattle

In memory of Tommy Monahan

Kathy Vorwick, president of the Greenbelt Nature Conservancy, performed the dedication ceremony with these words:

"To Tommy—We dedicate this place, this dock at Walker Pond, to the honor and memory of Tommy Monahan, a child of God, on the occasion of his tenth birthday.

Tommy loved all creation. He loved all the critters, including the four legged variety and those who crawled and swam. His eyes were open to wonder and new discoveries. He found joy in turning over a rock to see what lives underneath, in putting a net in the water to see what lives there.

May all who pass this place pause and feel of Tommy's spirit. May we, and those who follow, be inspired by the natural world Tommy so loved, by Tommy's example, and promise him that we will protect and cherish our part of paradise."

What a tribute to anyone, but to think he was only nine years old just boggles your mind. What an honor, but it truly doesn't surprise us. First a tree, then a star, a school courtyard, paintings in both a Brooklyn and a Staten Island school, an animal shelter, Skunk's Pond, now a magnificent dock, and next a park bench at Lemon Creek—in four different Staten Island locations, outside of Yellowstone National Park, and out in the galaxy.

We believe there was a purpose to Tommy's death. We try making sense out of it. Maria reports one of his teachers saying there was never enough time in the day to confirm all that Tommy knew. He was always filled with facts about nature and animals that were beyond his years. Some things he instinctively knew. Maria remembers looking him in the eyes, intently, and asking him, "Where do you come from? Who sent you here?"

The first time Tommy met Red Storm, the Native Americans who came to the conference house to educate the community about their culture, he was overjoyed. The entire time the Red Storm Drum and Dance Troupe performed, Tommy sat staring at them. He appeared to be mesmerized, as though he was seeing something familiar to him. He did not want to leave the conference house that day. He was completely absorbed in everything he saw and heard, and all he talked about that night was the information he learned that day.

When Maria and Tom began planning the events of his tenth birthday, they thought how nice it would be to have one of the Native Americans at the dedication of the dock. Maria called Robert Bold Eagle with their request. He asked permission to invite others from their troupe because they all knew about Tommy Monahan and wanted to participate.

Following the dedication of the dock, Robert Bold Eagle, his wife Marjorie, and his young son Running Horse invited Maria, Tom, and Gabrielle onto the dock with them. Robert gave us permission to share with you what he said prior to their blessing of the dock. He hesitated, clearing his throat and saying how emotional he was to be here for this little boy's celebration.

"Red Storm was invited here today, but the truth is, Tommy and his family has honored Red Storm by inviting us. Tommy's mother Maria told us that Tommy had seen us at a couple of our educational presentations. His mother Maria said he was completely in awe of what he was seeing and when the day was over he was still talking about what he learned. Tommy had a huge respect for the Native American culture and nature, all animals included. This respect for our culture and for the Creator's creations and especially the fact that Red Storm has touched Tommy's life in some way is how he honors Red Storm."

Tom, Maria, and Gabrielle were asked to participate in Red Storm's "blessing of the dock to make it a safe place." Robert Bold Eagle spoke in their native tongue. It was a beautiful ceremony. Red Storm then led all of us over a short bridge spanning the creek into a clearing in the woods, where they performed two rituals on the huge drum in memory of Tommy. Red Storm made the drum out of buffalo skin. They invited

Tom and Bobby Ryan to participate in their second drum ritual. Chills ran down my spine, and the tears just flowed. One of Tommy's friends reached out to my tears with a gentle touch saying, "It's okay." I knew how ecstatic Tommy was watching over all of us.

Some of our family members were facing toward the pond. Through the woods, they noted a beautiful moment at the end of the first drum ritual. The heron slowly flew up into the air, close to the trees, gliding around the perimeter of the pond three times like a corkscrew touching the leaves of the trees, and then flew off over the woods. It seemed the bird was a part of the ceremony. Who knows for sure?

Craig told Red Storm what he witnessed, convinced the heron was Tommy. Red Storm's reply was, "Yes, I know. There were many spirits with us today." It was a most memorable event.

Since we were unable to take pictures during the ceremonies out of respect for the solemnity of their service, Red Storm posed for us and with us at our request after answering our many questions about their culture. They returned to the conservancy with us, where we all shared in refreshments. It was a beautiful place to end a beautiful (although painful at times) day. This was the spot Tommy learned some of what he knew. This is where he met Atka, the wolf.

An interesting tidbit: Robert Bold Eagle's wife Marjorie is a descendant of the Lenape tribe, who lived and fished in Lemon Creek. Is it any wonder that Tommy's favorite playing grounds were at Lemon Creek? We now understand why he was drawn to Lemon Creek. We look forward to sitting on his bench there one day.

Maria shared Tommy's astrological sign of Virgo, an earth sign. If you believe in numerology, he was an "11." Elevens are considered ascended masters who come to earth to teach, not to learn. Who knows?

Melissa e-mailed the pictures she had taken at Walker Pond to a friend in California. Her friend enlarged the picture of the heron standing in the pond. He sent it back to Melissa after circling a section in the trees in the direction that the bird's beak was pointed, three feet above the bird. When looking carefully at that spot, some see the head and shoulders of Tommy, detecting his mouth and eyes. Once spotted, it's easy to see.

Terry was disturbed when she heard about this. All she could think about was, "What is he doing all alone in the woods?" She couldn't bear thinking of him all alone in the dark woods. Unable to shake her feelings free, she returned to the pond alone one day. While reflecting, she told Tommy, "I don't want you to be here alone." In the silence she stood, crying alone, except for the ladybug she noticed that had landed on her arm.

About twenty minutes into her crying, she heard the water moving, and then she heard a frog jumping up out of the water. She watched and listened. After a minute, about thirty frogs were on top of the lily pads. She couldn't believe what she was seeing and hearing. The frogs were leaping from one pad to another, all the while croaking. Then she saw a turtle head peeking up from under the water. She was beginning to feel peaceful with him being there.

All of a sudden, a dragonfly flew all around her. Tommy loved dragonflies. At this point, a second ladybug was tickling the back of her leg. By now her fears and anxieties about Tommy being alone were gone. She felt so peaceful, calm, and connected to him. As she walked the path back to her car, the first ladybug returned to the pond while the second ladybug remained on her leg. Terry said to Tommy, "Now I get it. Part of you remains here, and part of you comes with me." Terry drove to the other end of Staten Island to attend another nephew, Craig's, first soccer game. The ladybug on her leg attended Craig's game as well.

Tommy knew that whenever our family saw a ladybug, it was a sign to us that my mother in heaven was with us. She had loved ladybugs and never disturbed them when they were found in her house. She died in 1993. Tommy's parents bought her house, the house that was in the fire. They were still finding ladybugs in that house.

I strongly recommend you read *Water Bugs and Dragonflies* by Doris Stickney. It explains death to young children. In essence, the story explains how the water bug leaves the underwater world he knows to find out where his friends went after they climbed the lily stalk, never to return.

Cousins and friends on Tommy's dock at Walker Pond

Red Storm's Drum and Dance Troupe and Tommy's family

CHAPTER 15:
The Path to Acceptance

"May the Lord Himself who is our source of peace, give you peace at all times and in every way. The Lord be with you all."
(2 Thessalonians 3:16)

It's September 29 today. At this morning's Mass, I learned it is the feast day of the Archangels Michael, Gabriel, and Raphael. Until this morning, I couldn't understand why I had this date planted in my mind as the day I would finish writing this book. It turns out I will be finished writing it today.

There's no question in our minds that Tommy is an angel. St. Michael, our protector, please give our family strength to live our lives without Tommy in a way that makes him proud and protect us each and every day. St. Gabriel, our messenger, please guide us to listen to the Holy Spirit and help each other move into a full life of peace and service to others. St. Raphael, our healer, please send your healing powers to our broken hearts, especially Gabrielle, Tom, Maria, Ashley, and Kevin.

I am so grateful I decided to write this book. It has helped me tremendously to process my thoughts and feelings about our tragic loss of Tommy. I cry as I write these words. You see, writing helps, but it doesn't bring him back. My only consolation is my faith. I will see him again—and he is happy, I am sure of that. I am also fortunate to have seventeen other grandchildren to love.

I have written and rewritten my closing message to you all, but I believe I need to keep the message simple. My intention in printing this book is to reach out to others who struggle with their feelings as they try to make sense out of the death of a loved one, particularly a child. However, as I journeyed through this process, I found my faith being reinforced thanks to others' prayers for us, as well as the generosity and compassion bestowed on our family. Since Tommy's death, I have a greater respect for those who grieve in different ways. I can only share with you what works for me. My education and experience working with the bereaved for over ten years helped me accept the importance of respecting the different ways that people grieve. Tom and Maria shared with me that their anger at God was intense for letting them down. As parents, they couldn't understand why this happened to them. This is a normal emotion after the death of a child. I validate their feelings and pray they find their way through this reality.

Living with the death of a grandchild has been inconceivable, but less inconceivable because of my faith. Praying, swimming, sharing my feelings, and participating in life with my family and friends help me heal and bring some sense of peace to myself. This is an ongoing process. My way may not be your way, and my time is not your time. There is no time limit with grief. However, I hope sharing my way with you will help you find what works for you. Just know you are not alone …

If you struggle with your faith, don't give up. You deserve to be free of your pain. Search for a higher power that you can relate to and nourish that belief. Pray for guidance. I guarantee the Holy Spirit will never fail you. You just need to be open; open your mind and heart, and you will hear. When you let go of the negative thoughts and fears, you will absorb all the positive messages coming your way.

I thank all of you for sharing my journey with me. Please pray for our family. Please pray the rosary for Tommy.

I'll never stop grieving the loss of Tommy, but I hope to deal with this grief in a positive way. I'm better now at turning a negative into a positive. Negativity drains me; being positive energizes me. I pray that each and every one of you who struggle with these issues can benefit from my experience. Don't ever minimize the power of prayer. During my very low moments or days, I'd ask friends to pray for me. I know they did, because all of a sudden I would feel lifted in prayer. Thank you for your prayers. They worked for me. It's impossible to list the names of all of you who have been there for me these past nine months. I don't know how I would have gotten through in one piece without your prayers, words of comfort, and reminders that you are there for me. God bless you and all your families. May peace always follow you and your families.

I've chosen to end this book with the poem written by our friend Pat Cameron's daughter, Eileen. Her message is profound.

IN MEMORY OF TOMMY MONAHAN
Even though I have never met you,
I mourned the loss of your life like so many others,
Especially when contemplating just how young you were.
Even though I didn't know you, I later learned how you lived
And sadly how your death was a mirror of the short life you lived.
From the very beginning and until the end,
You lived your life trying to preserve the lives of those around you.
In just nine brief years, you lived more life
And did more good for humanity, animals, and the earth itself
Than most people have done or will do throughout their entire lives.
Throughout your existence you looked at the world
With a sense of discovery, innocence, and wonderment.
You viewed nature with passion and a sense of newness
As though you were looking at the world for the first time.
You looked at the earth and wildlife with the intensity of an explorer,
Which would come to define you for loved ones and strangers alike.
In celebration of your life and in honor of your memory,
I can only hope that all of the world and future generations
Will have a deeper respect for people and all living things in general,
Especially the animals that you so fervently cherished and respected.
Tommy, you were an extraordinary young boy
And through your own example of trying to rescue your pets,
People will continue your legacy
By donating money to animal shelters
And working toward the preservation of wildlife
and almost extinct animal species.
Even though I never met you,
I write these words in contemplation
Not of the lives that were lost,
But of the life that you lived
And what it meant to so many people,
Especially those whom you have never met.
Love and Prayers ... Eileen Cameron

The *Thomas Paul Monahans*

The five Thomas Paul Monahans—Grandpa, Tommy,
Dad, Great-Grandpa, Great-Great-Grandpa

Dad, Tommy, and Grandpa

Epilogue

On the Monday afternoon that I finished writing this book, I had an experience I would like to share with you. My last page was written at approximately three o'clock in the afternoon. When I picked up my paper to review what I had written, the sun was shining brightly through my window onto the kitchen table where I was sitting. As I read my final words, the tears just flowed from my eyes. I was overcome with emotion as my hands began to tremble. *I sensed Tommy's presence.* I took a few deep breaths to settle down.

I gently placed my paper onto the table with my left hand and the pen a few inches to the right of the paper. I experienced mixed emotions: relief, gratitude, some sadness and anxiety. I talked to Tommy, telling him I hoped he liked my book and how much I loved him. Through my tears, I noticed a lightning bug crawl out from under the paper.

I knew the bug was Tommy. I have never seen a lightning bug in broad daylight, and certainly never in my house before. He stopped crawling when he reached my pen. While I continued to talk to him, he did not move. I told him I knew he was letting me know he was here with me on this journey, hopefully with approval. Tears continued as I picked him up with a tissue, explaining how he would be happier outside with his friends since there were no children to play with in here.

I took him onto our back deck and opened the tissue as I continued speaking to him. When he initially did not fly away, I told him he would always be in my heart. I assured him that finishing my book did not mean that I would stop talking to him on a daily basis. I hoped that he would always feel my love. I encouraged him to have fun with his friends. Then he flew away, turned around, and landed on my right shoulder. I reminded him my love would be there forever. He then flew off my shoulder and landed on my glass back door that leads to the kitchen. I laughed and smiling said, "Thanks, Tommy. I believe you are telling me you will always watch over me. Feel my hugs and kisses, sweetheart. I love you now and forever."

While sharing this experience with a friend, I questioned why he came in the form of a lightning bug. I immediately realized that the first page of this book is dedicated to all my grandchildren. I hoped they would always feel God's light shining through them. On my last page, Tommy came to me as a lightning bug—a clear demonstration of God's light shining through Tommy. God is so good!

AFTERWORD

On behalf of the South Shore Garden Club of Staten Island, President Gertrude Sokolowsky contacted Bonnie Williams, director of the Conference House Park, New York City Parks and Recreation. Together they arranged for a tree-planting ceremony in honor of what would have been Tommy's eleventh birthday. They chose a "Green Vase" Japanese Zelkova tree, most appropriate for the planting spot.

They chose the perfect resting spot for the tree, on the grounds of the Conference House near the pavilion overlooking the mouth of the Arthur Kill River. Our neighbor Joe Quinn did a perfect job securing the plaque to a large rock that Tommy's dad took from their yard to be used under the tree.

Gertrude was the master of ceremonies, referring to Tommy as "our youngest hero." Gertrude's youngest daughter, Lynn McNamara, took care of the details to make this event happen. The most meaningful and personal invocation was performed by our pastor, Monsignor Edmund Whalen. Lou Tobacco, our state assemblyman, spoke from his heart about how grateful he was to participate in this event for such a special boy. Borough President Jim Molinaro reminded us how touched he was by Tommy from the moment he entered the room at Tommy's wake. He was so impressed by the effects this little boy had on so many people. Tommy's mom, Maria, moved everyone through her description of the meaning of this tree in his name:

> *"It has been 628 days since the sun and the moon shone brightly and the stars sparkled clearly. It has been 628 days and 11 hours since my world was tilted slightly off its axis. The climb has been steep and long and sometimes seems endless, but with the help of*

old friends and new friends alike, we are slowly emerging from our hell. With the guidance of some very wise and compassionate friends, we are learning to focus more on the gifts and treasures that Tommy brought to our lives instead of the "What might have beens."

That is what we are doing here today on what should have been the start of his twelfth earth year. We came together to remember his most passionate quality—his love of nature. For those who knew him, you remember his excitement and pure zeal for the Earth, the sea, and all the creatures who inhabit it. His eyes were always open to wonder and new discoveries.

Being here at the Conference House Park makes this day all the more meaningful. You see, Tommy loved this place. He knew it was hallowed and sacred Native American ground. He came here often, to explore and learn and maybe even to remember from a life lived long ago. The South Shore Garden Club has asked us here today to honor his memory by planting a tree—the significance of a gesture that Tommy would have loved.

A tree means bringing shelter to a plethora of God's creatures, from birds and bats, to squirrels and chipmunks and the slithering, crawling kinds that Tommy found so appealing. It will also serve as a respite for all of Sophie's four-legged friends. A tree gives shade and shelter from the sun and rain. A tree provides fresh oxygen to the earth's atmosphere. A tree grows free and unchecked. Yes, he would have been pleased.

But for myself and my family who have been left behind, it will have special meaning too. It will provide us with a measure of the passing of time. Not for forgetting or the lessening of our pain, but perhaps a softening of it. It will provide us a gauge. As we watch the tree grow, so will our love for our boy and the intensity we feel of missing him.

Tommy knew that nature was a gift to be cherished, respected, preserved, and protected.

I thank you all for coming here and remembering him with us today. Again, we couldn't have survived the past year and a half without all of you. I hope that for you, having known Tommy inspires you to more appreciate and treasure the beauty of the natural world and Mother Earth that we all share.

I would like to close with the borrowed words of another bereaved mother, Elizabeth Edwards (written for her son Wade). She wrote these words about her son; I think they are perfect for mine:

> *'His mark will endure. The good we do really is eternal, as we had told him, and now that axiom is a charge to us—not just to keep his memory, but to live his life message. We know that we can never make sense of his loss. He had done it all right, his life didn't last as long as it should have, but we are thankful for what he left us and he left everyone he touched the better for knowing him. We stand a little straighter in his shadow.'*

Thank you."

Tom Delacey from the Red Storm Drum and Dance Troupe honored Tommy's tree by blessing it with a Native American prayer ceremony. It was very touching.

I am amazed that the garden club was so determined to plant something in Tommy's memory. I believe my deceased mother's spirit spurred their interest. They were unaware that my mother was treasurer in their club in the 1950s. She also shared a special interest in Japanese trees. I was president of the South Shore Children's Garden Club in 1953.

When my son Tom was young, he worked with his grandma in her garden. As a teenager, he bought his grandmother her favorite tree, a dogwood, and they planted it together in her front yard. As an adult, he and his wife Maria bought his grandparents' house. Their children, Tommy and Gabrielle, climbed that same dogwood tree while living in that house, the house of the fire. There are no coincidences; God is everywhere.

I find myself being so comforted at Tommy's tree. My husband and I enjoyed a magnificent concert sitting in front of his tree on July 3, 2010. We'd glance at his tree, the flag, the flowers, and Tommy's plaque as we watched and listened to the Staten Island Philharmonic Orchestra and the Helluva Choir on the pavilion while small boats passed by on the river. The sky was very blue, with white clouds drifting by. What a perfect setting. We knew Tommy was with us as we listened to the patriotic music from the Civil War to the present. God bless America! God is good!

About the Author

Patricia Monahan and her husband, Tom, have seven children and eighteen grandchildren. Pat was a Girl Scout leader, a den mother, a Babe Ruth baseball team mother, and actively involved in church and school activities until she began a career. She retired after twenty-seven years as a New York State Certified Alcohol Substance Abuse Counselor. She volunteered for eight years at a homeless women's shelter. Trained by the archdiocese of New York as a bereavement minister, she cofounded the bereavement ministry at St. Joseph-St Thomas Parish on Staten Island, New York, in January 2000.

On December 17, 2007, Pat's nine-year-old grandson, Tommy, perished trying to save his dog Sophie from their house fire. The world she had known ended abruptly. She wrote *To Thee We Do Cry* as her way to reach others whose faith may have been shattered following the loss of a loved one, as well as her way of keeping Tommy's memory alive.

CPSIA information can be obtained at www.ICGtesting.com
Printed in the USA
LVOW131308301212

313763LV00004B/518/P